BRAINWASHED
AND ANOINTED

BRAINWASHED
AND ANOINTED

THE STORY OF
AN EX-MORMON

CHRIS YEOMAN

FONTHILL

For my family

Do not go gentle into that good night...
Rage, rage against the dying of the light.

Dylan Thomas

Fonthill Media Language Policy

Fonthill Media publishes in the international English language market. One language edition is published worldwide. As there are minor differences in spelling and presentation, especially with regard to American English and British English, a policy is necessary to define which form of English to use. The Fonthill Policy is to use the form of English native to the author. Chris Yeoman was born and educated in the United Kingdom; therefore, British English has been adopted in this publication.

Fonthill Media Limited
Fonthill Media LLC
www.fonthillmedia.com
office@fonthillmedia.com

First published in the United Kingdom and the United States of America 2018

British Library Cataloguing in Publication Data:
A catalogue record for this book is available from the British Library

Copyright © Chris Yeoman 2018

ISBN 978-1-78155-667-2

Typeset in 10pt on 13pt Sabon
Printed and bound in Great Britain by CPI Group (UK) Ltd, Croydon CR0 4YY

CONTENTS

Introduction		7
Prologue		9
1	Golden	15
2	Like Chocolate Cake	19
3	'Incoming!'	23
4	Out of the Mouths of Babes	25
5	Not Even the Queen	29
6	Rabbit	32
7	Shark	37
8	Guilt	44
9	The Phoney War	48
10	The Haze	56
11	Roseville, CA	63
12	Panic	67
13	Broken	72
14	Home	76
15	The Devil Must Have Heard	80
16	The Samurai Summer	85
17	Sin, Repent, Repeat	88
18	History	96
19	You Have No Power Here	102
20	The Final Nail	108
21	Aftermath	118
Epilogue		127

Introduction

In early January 2017, I published a blog about my experiences with The Church of Jesus Christ of Latter-day Saints, after having my name officially removed from the Church's records. I always thought that if I ever did officially leave Mormonism behind, I would just go away quietly. I never imagined in a million years that I would talk so openly on social media about my problems with the religion. After all, it was the most important aspect of my life for twenty-seven years, and I used to detest people who left and felt the need to write something like this—go away quietly, why kick and scream? Well, I have done my damned (pun intended) best to tell my story in a way that is not bitter and full of resentment because who wants to read that? I would not even want to write it. Instead, I have tried to illustrate how the Mormon faith has affected me as a person and those around me. I hope I have achieved this, but only you can judge it (I am used to being judged).

There are two reasons why I have decided to write this book. The first is that it is a good way to clean out my closet and hope for closure, because even now, I am not convinced the conditioning will ever truly be out of my system. The second is the most important reason as to why. Since I published my blog and became a little more conversational about my church life on social media, many people contacted me to thank me for it. Some were ex-Mormons, some were Mormons who are struggling, but most, believe it or not, were non-Mormons. I have been told several times now that I really ought to expand on my blog and write a book about it all because it may resonate with people and help a soul or two along the way. I hope it does because then, my experiences had some purpose.

To be honest with you, dear reader, there are a lot of things in this book that I find embarrassing and humiliating now that I am not a Mormon, but I needed to be transparent so that you can see what religion can do to people.

If you are religious, or Mormon, my intention is not to offend you; I respect your freedom to believe in what you want and how you want, I just ask for the same courtesy. These were my experiences and as a result, they formed my opinions. I still have Mormon friends, and I hope at the end of this book I still do because you are great people.

Lastly, I have changed many people's names in this book for obvious reasons; I do not want to get sued—I mean, to respect their privacy. Anyway, knock knock.

Prologue

'Hi!' The door slammed shut.

Knock knock. 'Hi, I'm ...' The door slammed shut again.

Ding dong. 'Hi!'

'No thanks'.

Knock knock. 'Hi! How are you today? Good? That's great! I'm Elder Yeoman and this is Elder Taylor. We're from The Church of Jesus Christ of Latter-day Saints, and we're in the area today sharing a message about Jesus Christ. Do you have a moment to hear it?'

'That's right, the Mormons! No, no, we don't practice polygamy, that's a break-off group. No, quite sure, I only have one mum, ha-ha.'

'Nah, not Australian, I'm from England'.

'Okay, well thank you for your time'.

Ding dong. 'Nope, that's okay. I can see you're in your underpants, you get back to whatever you were doing'.

Knock knock.

'Good evening, sir, I'm Elder Yeoman and this is Elder Taylor. We're from The Church of Jesus Christ of Latter-day Saints, and we are hoping to share a message with you about Jesus Christ and his restored gospel on the earth today. Would you be interested in hearing about God's plan for you and how you and your family can be together forever?

'The basketball's on? Who's playing? Cool! Well, maybe we can come back another time? No? Okay then, enjoy the game'.

We called it a night. It had been a typical day for two young missionaries, dressed in dark suits, white shirts, and black name badges. We had prayed before we left that we would be guided to someone with an open heart, someone willing to hear the gospel. Did people not know that their eternal salvation was on the line? I mean, come on. One guy did not even care about how he could be with his family for time and all eternity because the game was on. Oh well, I would pray for them.

If nothing else, I hoped we had at least made a good impression for the Church. We looked smart and friendly, and I was getting used to forcing myself to be a 'Hi, how are you doing?!' kind of guy. It was not natural for me. I was quite shy, not to mention British. We are not like Americans. At times, I felt like a better opener would be, 'Alright mate, sorry to bother you, I know this is a bit awkward and random, but do you think we could come in and talk to you about the Church, if you're not too busy?' Then (I will call him Stan) Stan, would let us in and we would meet his wife and kids, sit down on a comfy chair, decline a cup of coffee, 'but a water would be nice', and get down to business. 'This is a lovely home you have.' Maybe I would look around the room and try to discover some of their interests to break the ice. I would ask the kids how old they are; do they enjoy school? Thought not.

'Anyway, do you mind if we open with prayer?' Great! Stan, can you say it, please? ... Haha, only joking, I'll do it. Dear Heavenly Father, we're grateful to have been able to meet this kind family and to be in their home to share your message with them. Please send us your Spirit to testify of the truthfulness of the gospel. We are thankful for your blessings, and for this opportunity to be able to talk with this family about the importance of the Church, in the name of Jesus Christ, Amen.'

It felt slightly uncomfortable at first, but a quiet time-out for prayer had created a revenant atmosphere. I had everyone's attention now, and so I began to tell them about the first Latter-day Saint prophet, Joseph Smith.

Can you picture for a moment a world rife with religious confusion? That should be easy because it is one of life's constants. Let us narrow it down to your own city or town. How many churches are there? Think about how contradicting they all are. Think about all the different faiths, and how they all have their own different interpretations of the scriptures. How many of them are claiming to be the true church? How can you possibly know which church is God's true church when there are so many laying claim?

There was a fourteen-year-old farm boy called Joseph, who had also been feeling the frustration of all of the religious confusion. Some of his family members were Presbyterian, but he had been leaning towards the Methodist faith. It was all so bewildering for such a young lad. Joseph believed in God, but he felt like he was in religious darkness, until one day, a Bible verse lit him up like a firework. James 1:5 reads: 'If any of you lack wisdom, let him ask of God, that giveth to all men liberally, and upbraideth not; and it shall be given him.'

This passage of scripture was the answer to the dilemma. The verse says that he can ask God himself. He did not need to rely on his parents for answers; he did not need to trust in the local preachers anymore either—he could find out first-hand. So, after much pondering and reflection, that was exactly what young Joseph did.

The following extract is from the *History of Joseph Smith: the Prophet*, Chapter 1: 14–26, the 1838 account of the First Vision, which is said to have occurred in 1820, in a wooded grove near Joseph's family home in Palmyra, New York.

The Smith Family Log Home, Palmyra, NY, 2003

14 So, in accordance with this, my determination to ask of God, I retired to the woods to make the attempt. It was on the morning of a beautiful, clear day, early in the spring of eighteen hundred and twenty. It was the first time in my life that I had made such an attempt, for amidst all my anxieties I had never as yet made the attempt to pray vocally.

15 After I had retired to the place where I had previously designed to go, having looked around me, and finding myself alone, I kneeled down and began to offer up the desires of my heart to God. I had scarcely done so, when immediately I was seized upon by some power which entirely overcame me, and had such an astonishing influence over me as to bind my tongue so that I could not speak. Thick darkness gathered around me, and it seemed to me for a time as if I were doomed to sudden destruction.

16 But, exerting all my powers to call upon God to deliver me out of the power of this enemy which had seized upon me, and at the very moment when I was ready to sink into despair and abandon myself to destruction—not to an imaginary ruin, but to the power of some actual being from the unseen world, who had such marvellous power as I had never before felt in any being—just at this moment of great alarm, I saw a pillar of light exactly over my head, above the brightness of the sun, which descended gradually until it fell upon me.

17 It no sooner appeared than I found myself delivered from the enemy which held me bound. When the light rested upon me I saw two Personages,

whose brightness and glory defy all description, standing above me in the air. One of them spake unto me, calling me by name and said, pointing to the other—This is My Beloved Son. Hear Him!

18 My object in going to inquire of the Lord was to know which of all the sects was right, that I might know which to join. No sooner, therefore, did I get possession of myself, so as to be able to speak, than I asked the Personages who stood above me in the light, which of all the sects was right (for at this time it had never entered into my heart that all were wrong)—and which I should join.

19 I was answered that I must join none of them, for they were all wrong; and the Personage who addressed me said that all their creeds were an abomination in his sight; that those professors were all corrupt; that: 'they draw near to me with their lips, but their hearts are far from me, they teach for doctrines the commandments of men, having a form of godliness, but they deny the power thereof.'

20 He again forbade me to join with any of them; and many other things did he say unto me, which I cannot write at this time. When I came to myself again, I found myself lying on my back, looking up into heaven. When the light had departed, I had no strength; but soon recovering in some degree, I went home. And as I leaned up to the fireplace, mother inquired what the matter was. I replied, 'Never mind, all is well—I am well enough off.' I then said to my mother, 'I have learned for myself that Presbyterianism is not true.' It seems as though the adversary was aware, at a very early period of my life, that I was destined to prove a disturber and an annoyer of his kingdom; else why should the powers of darkness combine against me? Why the opposition and persecution that arose against me, almost in my infancy?

21 Some few days after I had this vision, I happened to be in company with one of the Methodist preachers, who was very active in the before mentioned religious excitement; and, conversing with him on the subject of religion, I took occasion to give him an account of the vision which I had had. I was greatly surprised at his behavior; he treated my communication not only lightly, but with great contempt, saying it was all of the devil, that there were no such things as visions or revelations in these days; that all such things had ceased with the apostles, and that there would never be any more of them.

22 I soon found, however, that my telling the story had excited a great deal of prejudice against me among professors of religion, and was the cause of great persecution, which continued to increase; and though I was an obscure boy, only between fourteen and fifteen years of age, and my circumstances in life such as to make a boy of no consequence in the world, yet men of high standing would take notice sufficient to excite the public mind against me, and create a bitter persecution; and this was common among all the sects—all united to persecute me.

23 It caused me serious reflection then, and often has since, how very strange it was that an obscure boy, of a little over fourteen years of age, and one, too, who was doomed to the necessity of obtaining a scanty maintenance by his daily labor, should be thought a character of sufficient importance to attract the attention of the great ones of the most popular sects of the day, and in a manner to create in them a spirit of the most bitter persecution and reviling. But strange or not, so it was, and it was often the cause of great sorrow to myself.

24 However, it was nevertheless a fact that I had beheld a vision. I have thought since, that I felt much like Paul, when he made his defense before King Agrippa, and related the account of the vision he had when he saw a light, and heard a voice; but still there were but few who believed him; some said he was dishonest, others said he was mad; and he was ridiculed and reviled. But all this did not destroy the reality of his vision. He had seen a vision, he knew he had, and all the persecution under heaven could not make it otherwise; and though they should persecute him unto death, yet he knew, and would know to his latest breath, that he had both seen a light and heard a voice speaking unto him, and all the world could not make him think or believe otherwise.

25 So it was with me. I had actually seen a light, and in the midst of that light I saw two Personages, and they did in reality speak to me; and though I was hated and persecuted for saying that I had seen a vision, yet it was true; and while they were persecuting me, reviling me, and speaking all manner of evil against me falsely for so saying, I was led to say in my heart: Why persecute me for telling the truth? I have actually seen a vision; and who am I that I can withstand God, or why does the world think to make me deny what I have actually seen? For I had seen a vision; I knew it, and I knew that God knew it, and I could not deny it, neither dared I do it; at least I knew that by so doing I would offend God, and come under condemnation.

26 I had now got my mind satisfied so far as the sectarian world was concerned—that it was not my duty to join with any of them, but to continue as I was until further directed. I had found the testimony of James to be true—that a man who lacked wisdom might ask of God, and obtain, and not be upbraided.

Elder Taylor and I would read from Joseph Smith's account rather than retell the story in our own words because the First Vision account, as it is known, is regarded as sacred scripture in the Church. If Stan and his family were willing to take on some verses too, even better, because the shared experience would invite the Holy Ghost into the room and into our hearts to testify to the truthfulness of the words by filling our souls with feelings of joy and warmth.

To really add to the impact of the message, I would share my own testimony with them. 'If I may, I'd just like to bear my testimony by saying that I know that Joseph Smith saw our Heavenly Father and His son Jesus Christ in the grove that

The Sacred Grove, Palmyra, NY, 2003.

day. I know this because just like Joseph, I asked God myself through prayer, and the Holy Spirit filled my heart with warmth, confirming it to be true. Following the ministry of Christ's apostles, and the apostasy that occurred, the world was in a state of spiritual darkness, but through Joseph Smith, God has restored his one true gospel upon the earth.'

Elder Taylor would then strengthen my testimony by sharing his own and we now relied on God to take care of the rest. Inwardly, I was praying that this wonderful family would recognise the Spirit, that they would feel this warmth and conviction in their own hearts, and know that what we were saying was the truth. We were not salesman trying to dupe anyone. We 100 per cent believed this in our hearts. We did not get paid to do this either. In fact, I had left my family and friends back in England to bring the gospel of Jesus Christ into people's lives.

We had just 'laid the smack down', as my companion liked to say (he must have been a fan of 'The Rock'). You see, we were encouraged to share our testimony as often as we could because no matter who you are, the Holy Ghost will always bear witness to the truth, and then, it was down to the individual to accept it or reject it.

'What a fascinating story, and what compelling young men. And do you want to know the best part about all of this? You don't have to rely on my testimony, you can ask God yourself and through his Spirit, you'll get the answer.'

'So, Stan and fam, what do you think?'

1

Golden

When I was about two years old living in South Farnborough, there was a knock at the door. Two missionaries from The Church of Jesus Christ of Latter-day Saints stood in the doorway and made their opening pitch to my dad. One of the young men was from South Africa and the other was from the States. My dad invited them in because he was curious about their message.

Ever since he was a young boy, Dad had always believed in God. He would often take himself off to the woods to pray. When he was only seven years old, he lost his father, which made for a tough upbringing. Prayer helped him to feel connected to his dad.

When the missionaries came knocking, Dad was a member of the Church of England, but he could see flaws in the religion, and he had been actively researching other faiths. Dad was working hard as a husband and a new father to put food on the table and a roof over our heads, but he was also suffering from panic attacks. He was desperately looking for something to alleviate his stress. What a perfect candidate for enthusiastic missionaries looking for souls to bring unto Christ.

Now, when I say this, it sounds sinister, but I do not mean it like that. I know these two missionaries had good intentions because we are still in contact to this day. They are good people and I know they did not even know of the advantage they had when they knocked on our door. Nevertheless, it is true that it is easier to influence someone who is feeling vulnerable than it is to do so to someone who is not. Dad was the golden investigator. He was interested in learning about religion, he was not deeply rooted in any one faith, and he was seeking comfort. Not only that, but when he heard about a young boy confused by religion praying in the woods, he could instantly relate.

Once my parents had learned about Joseph Smith's First Vision, they were introduced to the Book of Mormon. According to the Church, the Book of Mormon is 'Another Testament of Jesus Christ'. It is a book of scripture supposedly written on gold plates by prophets of old who lived in the ancient Americas. The heart of the book contains a visitation by the resurrected Christ, where he ministers to the people and rewards their faith in Him. The book ends with the last prophet, Moroni, burying the record in the Hill Cumorah, which is conveniently located just a few miles from where Joseph Smith would live in the 1800s—do not be too sceptical though as it was probably all part of the divine plan.

Three years after the First Vision, Joseph Smith recorded that he was visited by Moroni. The following extracts are from the *History of Joseph Smith: The Prophet* (Chapter 1, verses 27–35):

27 I continued to pursue my common vocations in life until the twenty-first of September, one thousand eight hundred and twenty-three, all the time suffering severe persecution at the hands of all classes of men, both religious and irreligious, because I continued to affirm that I had seen a vision.

28 During the space of time which intervened between the time I had the vision and the year eighteen hundred and twenty-three—having been forbidden to join any of the religious sects of the day, and being of very tender years, and persecuted by those who ought to have been my friends and to have treated me kindly, and if they supposed me to be deluded to have endeavored in a proper and affectionate manner to have reclaimed me—I was left to all kinds of temptations; and, mingling with all kinds of society, I frequently fell into many foolish errors, and displayed the weakness of youth, and the follies of human nature; which, I am sorry to say, led me into divers temptations, offensive in the sight of God. In making this confession, no one need suppose me guilty of any great or malignant sins. A disposition to commit such was never in my nature. But I was guilty of levity, and sometimes associated with jovial company, etc., not consistent with that character which ought to be maintained by one who was called of God as I had been. But this will not seem very strange to any one who recollects my youth, and is acquainted with my native cheery temperament.

29 In consequence of these things, I often felt condemned for my weakness and imperfections; when, on the evening of the above-mentioned twenty-first of September, after I had retired to my bed for the night, I betook myself to prayer and supplication to Almighty God for forgiveness of all my sins and follies, and also for a manifestation to me, that I might know of my state and standing before him; for I had full confidence in obtaining a divine manifestation, as I previously had one.

30 While I was thus in the act of calling upon God, I discovered a light appearing in my room, which continued to increase until the room was lighter than at noonday, when immediately a personage appeared at my bedside, standing in the air, for his feet did not touch the floor.

31 He had on a loose robe of most exquisite whiteness. It was a whiteness beyond anything earthly I had ever seen; nor do I believe that any earthly

thing could be made to appear so exceedingly white and brilliant. His hands were naked, and his arms also, a little above the wrist; so, also, were his feet naked, as were his legs, a little above the ankles. His head and neck were also bare. I could discover that he had no other clothing on but this robe, as it was open, so that I could see into his bosom.

32 Not only was his robe exceedingly white, but his whole person was glorious beyond description, and his countenance truly like lightning. The room was exceedingly light, but not so very bright as immediately around his person. When I first looked upon him, I was afraid; but the fear soon left me.

33 He called me by name, and said unto me that he was a messenger sent from the presence of God to me, and that his name was Moroni; that God had a work for me to do; and that my name should be had for good and evil among all nations, kindreds, and tongues, or that it should be both good and evil spoken of among all people.

34 He said there was a book deposited, written upon gold plates, giving an account of the former inhabitants of this continent, and the source from whence they sprang. He also said that the fulness of the everlasting Gospel was contained in it, as delivered by the Savior to the ancient inhabitants;

35 Also, that there were two stones in silver bows—and these stones, fastened to a breastplate, constituted what is called the Urim and Thummim— deposited with the plates; and the possession and use of these stones were what constituted 'seers' in ancient or former times; and that God had prepared them for the purpose of translating the book.

I know the Urim and Thummim part need not be explained because everyone knows what they look like and how they work, right? Or do you need the Urim and Thummim to help you translate that vague description? I doubt even Google can help. Anyway, the Church teaches that with these tools and through gifts of the Spirit, Joseph Smith was able to translate the ancient text referred to as 'ancient Egyptian', and his buddy, Oliver Cowdery, acted as scribe.

Of course, there is a lot more to this story, but in a nutshell, the Book of Mormon (named after the prophet Mormon, who abridged the record in ancient times) was published in 1830. Since then, the Book of Mormon has been printed many times over making copies readily available for anyone who would like one, free of charge.

I do not even need to check with my parents because I know the missionaries would have testified to the truthfulness of the Book of Mormon before they handed them a copy of the book for them to read. They would have shared Moroni's promise too (Moroni 10: 3–5):

3 Behold, I would exhort you that when ye shall read these things, if it be wisdom in God that ye should read them, that ye would remember how

merciful the Lord hath been unto the children of men, from the creation of Adam even down until the time that ye shall receive these things, and ponder it in your hearts.

4   And when ye shall receive these things, I would exhort you that ye would ask God, the Eternal Father, in the name of Christ, if these things are not true; and if ye shall ask with a sincere heart, with real intent, having faith in Christ, he will manifest the truth of it unto you, by the power of the Holy Ghost.

5   And by the power of the Holy Ghost ye may know the truth of all things.

Again, 'don't take our word for it, ask for yourself'.

I have pondered these verses so many times in my life to the point that I could quote them off by heart. I was raised Mormon, so the Church's doctrine seemed as natural to me as anything else I had learned about life. I was raised to believe that the Book of Mormon was the word of God, just like the Bible, and that Joseph Smith was a prophet of God, someone to be revered. So, because I grew up with the truth, Moroni's promise did not really apply to me; that was what I thought until someone told me that I ought to take up the challenge anyway and gain a personal testimony rather than the one I had been given by my parents.

In my teenage years, I used to put this to the test a few times. I had read parts of the book, studied Moroni's words, and done what was required to have the truth manifested to me by the Holy Ghost. I had felt pretty good at first, but maybe that was because it starts with, 'if it be wisdom in God that ye should read them?'

Straight away, I felt important. God's wisdom had allowed little old me to have access to this book, or maybe it was because it then asks for me to remember good things, like how merciful the Lord has been. I would think about how the Lord has blessed me with great family, close friends, and to be one of the rare kids in the Latter-days to be pretty much born into the true gospel. I would carry these good feelings into my prayer and think it was the spirit telling me that it was all true, but deep down, I would know that I had not really got definitive confirmation to my actual question, 'Are these things not true?' I would not say that this ever caused any serious doubt for me because soon after, when I voiced my concern, someone else told me that the reason God is not telling me it is true is because I already know it is. Why would God tell me something I already know? How silly of me. So that was why—now, stop bothering the Lord with this already.

When the missionaries left after their first discussion, I know that Dad prayed and eventually believed that he got a testimony that Joseph Smith was a true prophet, called by God to restore His gospel. So, if Joseph Smith was a prophet, then that made the Book of Mormon true as well, did it not? My Mum did the same, although it took her a little longer to be convinced.

2

Like Chocolate Cake

Conversion does not usually occur after just one visit from the missionaries. After their 'first discussion', they will keep coming back until they have taught you all about the gospel and what it requires of you to join. If all goes well after the first visit, you would have read some of the Book of Mormon, prayed about it, and hopefully 'felt' that it is a true book of scripture.

Sometimes, when I have been present while missionaries have been teaching someone, I have heard conversations like this:

'So, did you get a chance to read some of the Book of Mormon yet?'

'Yeah, I've read a couple of chapters'.

'Fantastic, and did you pray about the book?'

'Not yet, I've only read a little bit'.

'Well, you don't need to read all of it to know of its goodness. It's like if you have a piece of chocolate cake—you know it's good, but you don't need to eat the whole cake to know that'.

Actually, Elder 'Impatient Pants', it is probably a good idea for someone to read the whole book before making up their mind about it and devoting their life to it, do you not think?

'But the chocolate cake analogy,'

Yeah, but I was once in a youth church lesson where the teacher showed us a batch of cookies she had baked and told us that some had dog turd in. She said just because they looked good did not mean that they were. I forget what she was trying to get at now. It was probably something along the lines of 'just because something looks appealing, it doesn't mean it's good for you spiritually'. We thought she was just joking to make a point, but at the end of class, we asked if we could eat the cookies and she told us, 'No! Some really do have dog poo in'.

I am cherry picking verses here, so forgive the lack of context, but it furthers my point. Here is a passage from one of my favourite characters in the Book of Mormon, Nephi (2 Nephi 33:12–13):

12 And I pray the Father in the name of Christ that many of us, if not all, may be saved in his kingdom at that great and last day.

13 And now, my beloved brethren, all those who are of the house of Israel, and all ye ends of the earth, I speak unto you as the voice of one crying from the dust: Farewell until that great day shall come.

What a great attitude, Nephi. He hopes that everyone can make it to Heaven; I love that. There is no judgemental elitism, no doom and gloom. Instead, he is praying and hoping that everyone can be saved into the Kingdom of God; as one crying from the dust, that is just beautiful—what a great heart. I wish all religious people were like that.

However, in 2 Nephi 5:21–23, the verses are not as pleasant:

21 And he [God] had caused the cursing to come upon them, yea, even a sore cursing, because of their iniquity. For behold, they had hardened their hearts against him, that they had become like unto a flint; wherefore, as they were white, and exceedingly fair and delightsome, that they might not be enticing unto my people the Lord God did cause a skin of blackness to come upon them.
22 And thus saith the Lord God: I will cause that they shall be loathsome unto thy people, save they shall repent of their iniquities.
23 And cursed shall be the seed of him that mixeth with their seed; for they shall be cursed even with the same cursing. And the Lord spake it, and it was done.

Holy racism, Batman. You mean to say that the baddies who were once white and delightsome are now cursed to be black, so that they will not be enticing for the good white folks? Also, if the goodies do mix with the black baddies, they shall also be cursed? That sounds just as racist as the Bible. Wait though, this all sounds so much worse in this day and age. Was this even a problem for Americans in the 1800s, or was society back then equally as racist? We know the answer to that one. I doubt anyone even flinched at these verses back then; if anything, some people probably felt justified for their racist attitudes.

This 'cursed' group of wicked people in the Book of Mormon were called Lamanites. Growing up, I was taught in church that it was from the Lamanites that the Native Americans descended. I used to think that was some kind of physical evidence to authenticate the Book of Mormon, but when you think about it, what a farce; not only were the Native Americans butchered and driven from their lands by the white man, but now thanks to the Book of Mormon, they have white man writing their origin story about being a wicked, cursed, and loathsome people—thanks for the extra salt in the wound.

Church history tells us that there was never any segregation policy between black and white members in its congregations. Anyone was welcome to be baptised into the Church and to worship freely, but perhaps due to the social climate, or a more troubling philosophy (which I will get back to), black men were not permitted to be ordained to the priesthood. Black men and women could not enjoy the temple ordinances like white members did either. I must add that during Joseph Smith's lifetime as a prophet, a few black men were ordained to the priesthood, but following his death, his successor Brigham Young declared in 1852, that men of black African descent could no longer be ordained to the priesthood. This did not change in the Church until 1978.

I have actually heard people say, 'That's just how it was back then', to which I always ask: If God is a supreme being of infinite intelligence, wisdom and foresight, then why was His view on race not even at the maturity level of a twenty-first century human thinker? Or were prophets not actually receiving revelation about this from God? Is this just man's doing?

The idea that black skin is a curse from God originates from the Bible, in the book of Genesis. When Cain murdered his brother Abel, God put a mark on Cain and his decedents. This became known as the 'curse of Cain'.

In 1859 in Salt Lake City, Utah, Brigham Young remarked:

> You see some classes of the human family that are black, uncouth, uncomely, disagreeable and low in their habits, wild, and seemingly deprived of nearly all the blessings of the intelligence that is generally bestowed upon mankind. The first man that committed the odious crime of killing one of his brethren will be cursed the longest of anyone of the children of Adam. Cain slew his brother. Cain might have been killed, and that would have put a termination to that line of human beings. This was not to be, and the Lord put a mark upon him, which is the flat nose and black skin. Trace mankind down to after the flood, and then another curse is pronounced upon the same race—that they should be the "servant of servants;" and they will be, until that curse is removed; and the Abolitionists cannot help it, nor in the least alter that decree. How long is that race to endure the dreadful curse that is upon them? That curse will remain upon them, and they never can hold the Priesthood or share in it until all the other descendants of Adam have received the promises and enjoyed the blessings of the Priesthood and the keys thereof.

Brigham Young's *Journal of Discourses,* volume 7, pages 290–291

What a horrendous read, yet even in modern times, things were not much better. In 1958, Mormon Apostle Bruce R. McConkie published a book called *Mormon Doctrine*. This book was considered to be canon in the Church. My family even had a copy of it sitting on our bookshelf.

Mormons believe that we existed as spirits with God before we came down to earth to obtain mortal bodies. McConkie wrote that black people were less valiant in pre-existence and because of this, they were sent to earth through the lineage of Cain. Can you imagine having no recollection of a pre-earth life and being told that the reason you are black is because you were less valiant as a spirit than those who are born white? I have a friend who served a mission in Africa who had to try and help black members of the Church make peace with this absurd 'doctrine'.

I once asked a local church leader how it can even be possible. 'I mean, why in 1978 are black men suddenly deemed worthy to hold the priesthood by the Church?'

'Oh, well, all of the less valiant spirits would have come down to earth by then, so the only reason they are black now is a matter of biology, not because they have any curse'.

This racism is an embarrassment and a stain in Mormon history. I think a lot of Mormons appease themselves with chalking it all up to being the world's attitude at the time, but it has always bothered me that if the Church is directed by God himself, then they should have been ahead of the curve.

If you are not a member of the Church, then you may be wondering just how I ever dedicated my life to a church like this. I suppose the simple answer would be that I never learned about any of this in church. It is not something taught or promoted. In fact, the Church today has even rejected this racist doctrine taught by past leaders. Sure, I would come across verses every now and then about wicked people in the scriptures being cursed, but I never looked into it enough to understand how that even related to races and cultures today. I did not even have the internet back then, so it was only in my adult years that I began to learn of this shady history and I began to ask questions and do my own research. Even though the modern Church has shunned racist doctrines taught by past leaders, I wonder how they can still claim that those men were indeed called as prophets and apostles by God. How can you trust in these men if some of their teachings have since been rejected and cast out of official Mormon doctrine?

So, back to you, Elder 'Impatient Pants', maybe you should not tell people that the whole chocolate cake is just as tasty as the first bite.

3

'Incoming!'

Missionaries can be over zealous when they find a golden investigator because they want to strike while the iron is hot. It is the only purpose to their waking day on a mission. They will drive (if they are lucky), ride bikes, or walk all over the place trying to find people to teach. They know cold-calling is not the most effective way to bring souls unto Christ, but if the members are being lazy and not setting up their friends and colleagues for visits, then all they can do is knock doors or talk to people in the street. So, after hours of rejection, when someone does allow them in to teach, and they accept the challenges of reading the Book of Mormon with an open heart and to pray for an answer, they tend to get excited.

The first step is to get the investigator to feel the Spirit. If they recognise the fruits of the Spirit, namely the warm fuzzies, then everything else will be easier for them to swallow because there are some incoming bombshells.

Mormonism's foundation is Joseph Smith and the Book of Mormon. If you believe that God, the Father, and His son, Jesus Christ, appeared to Joseph Smith in the grove and later called him as a modern-day prophet to restore the true gospel on the earth, beginning with bringing forth the Book of Mormon, then surely you will accept everything else that follows.

My parents already believed in God, and although they were attending the Church of England, they knew that certain things were missing from their chosen faith. For example, the Church that Christ set up in his ministry consisted of twelve apostles. The Holy Bible was also full of prophets who spoke on God's behalf. Where were they today? Why should God stop communicating with mankind?

It must have been fascinating for my parents to learn that there was a prophet on the earth and there were also twelve apostles just like in Christ's time. In fact, the missionaries informed them that in 1829, God restored the priesthood authority to Joseph Smith and Oliver Cowdery by sending Peter, James, and John, in resurrected form, to ordain them to the priesthood by the laying on of hands, and on 6 April 1830, The Church of Jesus Christ of Latter-day Saints was officially established.

Missionaries and church investigators often form a close bond during the teaching period. My parents became good friends with the two missionaries who were paying them regular visits. Mum and Dad would cook for them, play board games with them, and got to know all about these young men and their lives back home. It was a real friendship that has lasted to this day. When my parents gained their testimonies that the Church was indeed true, the missionaries then taught them about some requirements which they would need to keep in order to be baptised. My companion and I referred to them as the bombshells, as you will see.

'As members of the Church we refrain from drinking alcohol, smoking, harmful drugs, we don't drink tea and coffee either, and you'll need to covenant to pay tithing to the Church. That's ten per cent of your earnings'.

I remember being astonished when a Sunday school teacher once told us primary kids that we ought to be paying 10p tithe on our £1 pocket money. We knew that 90p was not going to pay for 100 penny sweets, now was it?

I hated dropping tithing into the discussion when I was a missionary, but true converts accepted the spiritual law. The Church does not have paid ministry and I have mentioned before that missionaries do not get paid for their service. Tithing helps pay for church buildings, temples, books, manuals, and all sorts of things, but that does not make it any easier when asking people if they will commit to it.

In 1983, my parents were baptised into the Church and my two-year-old self was not too bothered about not being able to partake in drugs and alcohol, so I guess I went along with it.

4

Out of the Mouths of Babes

I was not a convert; I was raised by Mormon indoctrination, so nothing felt like a bombshell to me as a kid. It was all just so natural. Joseph Smith was as heroic to me as the Karate Kid or He-Man, as a youngster. Not being allowed to drink tea of coffee was also as normal to me as knowing not to down a pint of pond water.

The Church being true was never even a question for me growing up. Life was easy back then as a Mormon babe. Other than three hours (which felt like three months) at church on a Sunday, there was not much to it. Looking back though, I am not sure how healthy it is to start the conditioning that young. During a school week, I was singing 'The Wheels on the Bus', and on Sundays I was singing: 'I hope they call me on a mission, when I have grown a foot or two. I hope by then I will be ready to teach and preach and work as missionaries do.'

This is possibly my earliest association with missions. 'I hope they call me, I hope by then I will be ready ... and work as missionaries do'. Maybe that does not seem like much to you, but it was slightly intense for a child to be hoping for a mission call before even being able to dress itself properly.

Something else that I used to think was harmless while I was active but have since thought differently about is when children get up at a testimony sharing meeting and say things like: 'I know that Joseph Smith was a prophet, I know that the Book of Mormon is true.' It even bothers me now that grown adults declare 'I know'. No, you believe, or you have faith—you do not unequivocally 'know' at all. Even I was guilty of that. Your feelings cannot be relied upon as fact because they are liable to change. Yet to have children that still believe in Santa Claus and the Tooth Fairy repeating church mantras like that just seems off.

Another early memory I have regarding missions is being in a meeting where a soon-to-be missionary and his family were giving talks before his imminent departure. I remember knowing that he was leaving for two years and seeing his family in bits up at the pulpit. His sisters were sobbing their hearts out as they tried their best to seem happy about their brother leaving. I came home from church that day and went up into my bedroom and cried my eyes out. I remember my Dad coming in and asking me why I was so upset and I sobbed that I did not want to leave my family and go on a mission. Dad hugged me and said that I did not have to go if I did not want to and I soon calmed down.

My memories of primary are pretty vague now, but I met my lifelong best friends there. I do have one memory, however, which has stuck with me. I must have been about eight or nine years of age when a teenage girl in my street gave me this weird metal toy (for lack of a better word) of two people having sex. You would move a lever and a man's massive penis would thrust into the woman. I was fascinated by it, so I put it in my pocket and took it to church the next Sunday to show my best friend, Tim.

Once in primary, I remember handing it to Tim to look at, but I told him to make sure that he did not get caught. Tim's best idea for being discreet was to go and stand in the corner of the room with his face to the wall and have a go on the lever—that did not look conspicuous at all. After about thirty seconds, a primary teacher busted Tim and took the object off him. In a fluster, he said it was mine, so the teacher then approached me about it. I lied that I had found it outside in the chapel grounds before I came in and that I did not know what it was. She confiscated it but I think she bought the story. I worried all day that she would tell my parents, but I do not think she ever did. I remember worrying about it for a few days until I decided that the coast was clear, but I always felt awkward around this teacher for the rest of my days in that ward.

Me and Dad dressed in white at my baptism, 1989. LDS baptisms are done by full immersion. When Dad baptised me, he asked me how I felt; I said, 'Like I've been slimed'.

When Tim and I advanced from primary to youth classes, we tried our best to be invisible in the lessons we shared with the older, cooler kids. We were painfully shy, sensitive boys, and we inwardly died if we were called upon to give an answer or to read something out in front of everyone. Tim had a stutter, and my voice was breaking, so my tone would go from Barry White to Barry Gibb in the same sentence.

As much as we tried to stay invisible, we did not help ourselves because we would set each other off into fits of giggles, and church was the most inappropriate place to be laughing uncontrollably. We got so bad that we would have to stand outside the classroom for a while to compose ourselves.

When we reached the age of twelve, we were ordained into the Aaronic priesthood and became deacons. This meant that we would take up duties of passing the sacrament to the congregation on Sundays. The priests would bless the bread and water and we would take it around on metal trays so that those who were worthy could partake and renew their covenants with Christ. This is the most sacred part of the meeting, and the whole point of going to church, so it is a time for strict reverence. This is not a good time for giggly young men going through puberty. We would awake at the last possible moment on Sunday, quickly get dressed, eat some cereal, jump in the car, and arrive at church. Before we knew it, we were standing around the sacrament table, not long out of bed, trying to fend off unwanted morning glories; I swear we would get boners at the most inconvenient and inappropriate times. I remember trying to pin it back with a hymn book, or the sacrament tray, desperately willing it to go away. Luckily, our trousers were super baggy back in those days.

While the sacrament is being administered, most of the congregation are deep in reflection and prayer, so you can hear a pin drop. We would be doing our best not to look at each other because we knew we would set each other off, but every so often, someone in the congregation would slip an unplanned fart out and the battle to suppress our hysterics would begin. I would look everywhere I could but at the other deacons, yet out of the corners of my eyes, I could see their shoulders shaking up and down. On one occasion, one deacon accidently slammed his tray into someone's knee and the guy yelled out in pain. We all sounded like Muttley from *Wacky Races* that day.

Another moment that slayed us in church was when someone giving a talk quoted Exodus 20:17: 'Thou shalt not covet thy neighbour's house, thou shalt not covet thy neighbour's wife, nor his manservant, nor his maidservant, nor his ox, nor his ass, nor any thing that is thy neighbour's.' However, instead of saying 'ass', he said 'arse', and to make it worse, he went on to explain the scripture and said, 'you shouldn't covet your neighbour's arse'; my neighbour is a nice guy, but I do not think I have ever even looked at his arse.

There was also a time when the keyboard player fell asleep during someone's talk. He started to lean backwards in his chair and the legs gave out. As he was falling, he suddenly woke up and tried to use the keyboard to pull himself up. Dun, dun, dun on the keys, and I was a mess. I had to walk out of the hall and compose myself for about ten minutes.

I have saved the best story for last; even now, my friends and I still crease up over this one. There was a man in our ward that was super amped up when he talked. One Sunday, he stood up in church to berate the brethren about their home teaching figures.

Home teaching is a practice where priesthood holders are paired up and assigned families to visit once a month. They will share a spiritual message with the families they visit, and they also attend to any of the family's needs or help them with any problems they may have. It was a really great part of the Church to be fair, but people never seem to value the importance of it. Sure, people are busy, but from what I have seen, most people rush a visit at the end of each month just to tick the box because figures are collected by leaders. The women of the Church, who are part of the Relief Society, also do this, but it is called Visiting Teaching.

So, this one guy was complaining about it, but in a friendly kind of way, trying to hype the brethren up to take it more seriously and get out there and do it more often. The only thing was he substituted the word 'nag' and replaced it with 'bone'. With great enthusiasm, he exclaimed: 'I've been boning the Bishop for weeks over this, and now I'm going to bone all of you! After this, I'm going to head down to Relief Society and bone your wives too! And I'm going to keep on boning you until things improve!'

One of my friends recently said to me that being raised in the Church was all worth it for that one moment. I think that day caused my insides permanent damage.

The youth programme was not all just awkwardness and giggles. It did provide opportunities for some decent experiences that we may not have had outside of the Church back then. I remember spending a week in Yorkshire with a large group of the young men, where we went rock climbing, abseiling, and potholing. Tim and I got lost in York though and could not find our leaders for hours. We tried two lifelines; one was phoning Mum, but what could she do? All we did was tell her we were lost and just worried her sick. She did not hear back from me until a day or two later. The second thing we did was start praying to God that he would lead us back to everyone else. Eventually, we did come across some people from our group, and the drama was over. It had been our first time away from home. Tim and I were miserably homesick but we got each other through it. One of our youth leaders was the coolest guy we knew too. He would talk about girls with some of the older lads, and at night, when we would all settle down to sleep, he would play the Lisa Stansfield song, 'Time to Make you Mine'. He is in prison now for paedophilia.

5

Not Even the Queen

In my early teens as a Mormon, my self-importance started to bloom. Childish notions began to be packed away like my *Thudercats* figures, and I started to mature in the gospel. Our Sunday school teachers seemed stricter and more serious with us now, and I suppose I wanted to emulate my older peers too; they did not seem to think that fart jokes were funny anymore.

As I developed as an Aaronic priesthood holder, my duties extended to blessing the sacrament and home teaching. In classes, we were reminded just how blessed and privileged we were to be priesthood holders in today's world.

My friends and I grew up being told on a number of occasions that we were valiant spirits in the pre-mortal world and held back until these last and most wicked of days—we were the elect. I felt so bad for my less valiant school friends. I guess they were not as worthy as me back in the old spirit world, and that was why they were not born into a special Mormon family. 'Fear not though less valiant souls,' I thought, 'you have been blessed with me as a friend and so I will help you learn how to be saved.'

As young priesthood holders, we were told that we held the keys to the ministering of angels. This meant that we could call down angels if we needed. Believe me, I tried this all of the time, but it never happened. When I felt frustrated by not being able to achieve this, I used to tell myself that they were probably around, it was just that I could not see them.

I was also told so many times that 'not even the Queen has the authority you have. If the Queen was to come to church today, she wouldn't be able to bless the sacrament, but you can because you've been ordained'. That was a strange thing to say considering that not even Latter-day Saint women were allowed to bless the sacrament either.

The Church is extremely empowering for men. God is male, Christ is male, all the prophets and apostles are male, and only men are permitted to hold the priesthood. It is priesthood holders who lead the Church, both in Salt Lake City (Church HQ), and locally. The bishop is always male, as are his two counsellors. We know absolutely nothing about our Heavenly Mother because apparently 'she's too sacred to speak about, and God would not want her name being used in vain'. Women in the scriptures are also rarely spoken about. The Bible is terrible for this, but the Book of Mormon is even worse. The women do have their own organisation at church though: the Relief Society, which was formed by Joseph Smith's first wife, Emma. Other than at a Relief Society class at church on a Sunday, a priesthood holder is always present for their activities.

Sadly, when I was growing up, this was all just normal for me. The men were the patriarchs, and the priesthood was what made the Church tick. The men attended to church business, took care of the sacrament ordinances, and performed baptisms and confirmations. The Relief Society baked the cakes though.

This sexism did not go unnoticed in the Church. A nice little sweep-up line I have heard so many times is, 'Men need the priesthood; the women are naturally spiritually in tune'.

The young women were pretty much told that their purpose as daughters of God was to stay worthy and to marry a returned missionary. They were to be homemakers and have children. Not so fun fact: women do not even get called on a mission. Instead, they can volunteer if they feel prompted or are having trouble finding a husband. Women missionaries do not even serve for two years like the men either; apparently, eighteen months is enough—come on sisters, get home and start breeding.

I never once heard a career-promoting message for the women. Education was said to be important because that was something they could squeeze in before they started popping out little elect children. It was always all about becoming mothers and homemakers.

Another not so fun fact: in a temple session, the men and women are segregated. The women sit on the left side of the room and the men sit on the right. At one point, the women are asked to veil their faces too. My wife loved finding that out.

The day after I posted my blog about leaving the Church, one of the young women I grew up with thanked me for mentioning how they are programmed to marry a returned missionary. She felt the weight of this pressure and ended up marrying a returned missionary who was abusive. Fortunately, he is out the picture now and she is living out a much-loved career and in a happy relationship with a non-member.

The young men also feel an enormous pressure to serve a mission for fear that none of the girls will date them if they do not. When I was in the Missionary Training Centre, a couple of my roommates admitted that this was a major reason for them being there. It does not matter if you are the most kind-hearted, romantic, awesome guy, if you bailed on your mission call, then you were not the 'worthy returned missionary' candidate that they had been told to marry.

My friend Tim and I were useless around the girls at this age, but Tim had discovered some wisdom that I was yet to learn. In my journal, I wrote the following:

Me and [Tim] were speaking about beautiful girls and how after our missions that we'll date them. No one in particular because we don't know any. We were just dreaming. Anyway I said those kind of girls are way out of my league and he said to me that the only person that would stop me going out with gorgeous girls is me. He then said that he's going for girls that are out of his league because you have to be confident about yourself, and it works. You have to be positive and confident and enthusiastic, and if you get blown out...who cares? Keep trying and you'll succeed.

I roared with laughter when I read the pathetic line, 'No one in particular because we don't know any'. It is interesting to note my mindset though. After our missions, we will date them.

In the Church, you are not supposed to date anyone until you turn sixteen, and even then, it is supposed to be in groups. This probably works better in the US because dating seems to be more casual. In the UK, I would be called a player. Most of the girls my age at church were too busy swooning over prospective missionaries to even notice me, and so, I soon discovered that I was not going to be dating Mormon girls.

When I was about fifteen, I had my first serious girlfriend from school. Laura was not a Mormon, but she was respectful of my religion. I was probably getting close to being sixteen, so I do not recall any murmurings about it, not to my face anyway.

6

Rabbit

When I was growing up, I experienced some bullying from local kids for being Mormon. I think they would have bullied me even if I was not, but being Mormon did not help me to fit in with them. I was laughed at and called names for going to church, but it did not get to me that much. I knew I was elect and they were not. Being cornered and punched in the face a few times was a bitch though.

School was better for me. My classmates all knew I went to church but no one made me feel peculiar for it. In junior school, I remember really trying to sell how fun it was to my classmates by telling them that I get to draw superheroes the whole time while the grownups talk.

Other than not cursing like a sailor like the other kids who had started to learn swear words, I think I blended in just fine. Even secondary school was quite easy on me because the guys I used to hang out with did not really drink alcohol either. When I would go to parties, I was always made to feel welcome and included by people despite the fact that I did not join them in drinking alcohol. One guy told me, while people were getting smashed in a park on hooch, that I did not need alcohol to blend in because I was crazy enough already. I took that as a huge compliment that day—yay for being viewed as mental.

I never judged any of my schoolmates back then, and if I did privately, it was just because I was insecure about them growing away from me. In any case, these less valiant kids could not help it really, could they? They did not know any better.

I was lucky to have good friends around me and I managed to balance being Mormon-minded with blending in with civilian lifestyles. My younger brother was not as fortunate. He really took onboard being told as a primary child to express his beliefs to his school friends and invite them to church on Sunday, as if such missionary efforts would then convert his pubescent peers, who in turn would convert their parents, and then a whole new family would be baptised into the Church. Unsurprisingly, none of them came to church and my brother became a target for cruel bullying until he was finally forced to leave school early.

It is strange enough for people when they see you declining tea, coffee, and alcohol, to notice how you shy away from crude jokes, and to hear you using words like 'flip' instead of the F-bomb. It is noticeable when you decline playing football on a Sunday with your friends in the park because you are going to church for three hours in the morning and then keeping the Sabbath day holy for the rest of the week. Is there really any need at all to be telling young kids to be an example to their friends, to teach them about the Book of Mormon, and to invite them to come and pray and sing hymns with you on Sunday? Start them early, eh? Let them learn the robotic mantras before they form an opinion of their own. 'I know that Joseph Smith is a prophet, I know that, blah, blah, blah'.

You could teach them that the moon is a giant football that God kicked across space and they would bear their testimony about it. It was not a form of brainwashing though—how could it be when it was all true? If anything, parents are saving their children by getting them indoctrinated so early on—it was so noble.

I am sure there are plenty of people out there that suffered some form of unnecessary ridicule because they were told on a Sunday to be missionary-minded with their friends. I count myself lucky that I decided not to really push my beliefs on anyone. My friends knew I was Mormon and they respected my choices, and that was all that was needed back then.

I want to set the record straight in case my parents read this—I do not blame them at all for raising me like they did. They were never militant Mormons, but they were encouraging. I know they were doing what they thought best, but they were also under the captivating spell of religious delusion. I do not even hold the missionaries who converted them responsible either because they too were genuinely doing what they believed in, or were raised to do. I suppose the buck has to stop with the Church itself, the religion, and the leaders who continue to enforce its negative influence on people today.

It would be remiss of me to sit here tapping these laptop keys after a statement like that and not mention the good the Church as an organisation does in the world. It has a welfare programme that has benefited many people who have struggled. It has provided aid across the globe for decades. Mormon volunteers are often on site during world disasters and crisis. The Church also provides service in local communities, and is a safe haven for many people. There are fantastic Mormons who do a lot of good in the world, who take the time to uplift and support those in need. They give their time to enrich the lives of those around them and many members of the Church are generally decent human beings.

The negative influence I refer to is the dangerous indoctrination of the mind and the effects it can have on those who get sucked in by it. In due course, I will explain how Mormonism tore me to pieces as a person, but before that, allow me to set the scene.

When I was a teenager, my life was jam-packed with routine. My day would begin by waking up at around 6 a.m., throwing some clothes on, and waiting to be picked up for early morning seminary.

Seminary is basically an advanced scripture study class for the young, taught in the home of whoever was the teacher for the year. There is nothing more painful than listening to a group of tired youths droning their way through a hymn before the birds have even started singing. Pray, sing, listen to the lesson, have some breakfast, and get back home for personal prayer and scripture study, all before getting ready for school. Seminary was on four mornings of the school week for four years. Like a fool, I asked to do an extra year because I wanted to be more prepared for my mission.

On Monday evenings, we would have Family Home Evening. We would gather as a family to do much the same: pray, sing, read scriptures, and listen to the lesson one of us had prepared. Sometimes, we would end the evening with a game or a movie.

I cannot say I enjoyed seminary, especially in winter because it was freezing cold dragging myself out of bed to join my zombie class for a lesson we half took in. I remember one morning, the teacher asked me to read a scripture verse and with blurry eyes, I read: 'The same came to Jesus by night, and said unto him, Rabbit, we know that thou art a teacher come from God'.

The class burst out laughing and the teacher groaned, 'Come on, Chris, Rabbi, not rabbit!'

Seminary was definitely not my favourite pastime, but spending time with my family at Home Evenings was always worthwhile.

Tuesday evening was youth night, where activities ranged from playing sports, manhunt, or doing someone's gardening for them. Some nights were better than others. I remember always trying to cherry pick when I went, but it did not always work. I would be keen for basketball nights, but not so much for learning how to tie knots, or how to read a map.

Sunday was the usual three hours of church, and sometimes, an evening lesson called a 'fireside'. There was also a night in the week, once a month, where I would go home teaching with my Dad too. My Dad was a good home teacher, so at least he was not going to get 'boned' by that sex maniac at church.

It was a pretty intense schedule with school homework, seminary reading assignments, and a Sega Mega Drive. Mormonism really was a way of life, and the older I got, the more ingrained it became.

After Moroni's promise had failed to work for me, I came to the conclusion that I had always had a testimony that the Church is true. I resolved that by living the gospel, my faith would continue to grow, and as you can see from the following journal entry, I swallowed up the 'I know' mantras just for good measure.

When I pray I feel and recognise the Spirit more now than ever before. When I read the scriptures, the Spirit fills my heart and I know they are true. When I hear a talk, I know it's true. When I hear an apostle or the prophet speak, I know they speak the truth. When I home teach and share a message, I know it's true. Unlike some people I did not gain a final witness, or miraculous vision, or wonderful manifestation. My testimony came gradually. It came by 'doing'. The more I 'do', the stronger my testimony gets. I lived the gospel and kept the commandments first, and then the Spirit testified to me of the truth. Now I can say that the Holy Ghost has manifested the truthfulness of The Church of Jesus Christ of Latter-day Saints to me. In my heart the Spirit testifies to me and enlightens my soul, and I know that Christ is the head of our church. I know that Joseph Smith saw our Heavenly Father and Jesus Christ; I know The Book of Mormon is another testament of Jesus Christ. I know these things are so because the Holy Ghost shows to me that it is. Every time I think of these things, or write these things, or talk of these things, the Spirit testifies to me that they are true. It's like a fire burning in my soul and it just gets bigger and hotter. So I can say that I have a great witness, but the early stages were built by 'doing' it first and then came the witness. Live the commandments and then the witness will come.

Who is my teenage self trying to convince: you or me?

There is always a way out of unexplained situations in the Church. If a prayer does not get answered, then they chalk it up to God's mysterious ways. So, if for some reason, you have not got the right levels of faith for Moroni's promise to set your heart ablaze, then how about just living the gospel anyway? You would feel the Spirit eventually. I was also taught that the gaining of one's testimony can be found in the bearing of it. Is this not conditioning the mind in its most obvious form?

Just reel off those lines enough times until your brain accepts them as truth. It is like looking in the mirror before a job interview and telling yourself, 'You can do this'. You start to overcome the anxiety with positive belief. This is the same thing with encouraging people to bear testimony. Say a lie enough times and you will believe it. It is funny to me now how everyone's testimony sounds pretty much the same too.

Here's another journal entry of me trying hard to convince myself: 'Something that I liked from a talk by Boyd K. Packer, (Apostle) is that the Holy Ghost is so special and amazing that there are no actual words that describe how it feels.' That is convenient.

Sometimes it brings me joy, excitement, happiness, and confidence, and other times it touches me and I feel reverence and humbled. I think of the Lord and I feel like crying, and other times it comforts me, guides me, and testifies to me. I cannot find the right words.

If I was still a Mormon, I might read that and think to myself, 'See, Chris, you did recognise the Spirit', but I know that I have felt those exact emotions when I have watched a touching movie, or listened to a moving song. Joy, excitement, and happiness are not feelings exclusive to Mormonism either.

Most missionaries will tell investigators that when they are reading the scriptures to look out for feelings of love and warmth. 'These are the fruits of the Holy Ghost'.

If you are feeling vulnerable and you are reading about Christ's love and sacrifice for you, it is only natural to conjure up those feelings. I have had the same emotions when reading about the courage and sacrifices of soldiers in the Second World War. Other people can get those feelings when looking at art or reading Shakespeare. Again, there is always a way out. 'Yeah, they can. That's because everything good comes from God'.

7

Shark

Juggling church and school activities had its challenges, but it was the only life I knew back then. I was told that I would be blessed in my school studies if I attended seminary, but I am not sure that being tired all the time and splitting my homework with scripture reading was a winning combination for good grades.

In my teenage years, I noticed that some of my church classmates started to go missing in action. I guess primary songs and Sunday school lessons had not sunk in enough. They became more interested in drinking and girls and so I did not see them as much. I remember one lad leaning over to me and saying that one in four of us would go inactive. We counted all the boys who had stopped coming out on a Sunday and felt even more elect to still be sitting there.

When I was fifteen and attending seminary, church really became more serious to me. I think the intense study sessions really started to have an effect on my mind. The indoctrination became more forthcoming for someone who would be preparing for a mission in a few years' time too. I began a quest to read all of the scripture books from cover to cover and to learn as much as I could about Joseph Smith and church history. The more I began to educate myself away from classes, the more I also began to feel a heavier weight of responsibility to be perfect. I really wanted to always have the Spirit of God with me and to make it to Heaven, but it was not going to be as easy as that. My morals would be challenged by teenage life.

I have mentioned before some basic Mormon rules that set the religion apart from others. The Word of Wisdom, which Joseph Smith apparently received from God, forbade the Saints from smoking tobacco or drinking liquor and hot drinks. In those days hot drinks were tea and coffee. Some people believe that the reason we are meant to abstain from tea and coffee is because of the caffeine content, but all the revelation says is that hot drinks are not good for the belly. On a side note, this is why some members do not drink cola, but they still drink hot chocolate or eat chocolate bars—go figure.

I remember being in a priesthood lesson once where the teacher was telling us that Mormons should not drink cola. My family would always speak out against this because firstly, we enjoyed it, and secondly, because it was not doctrine. My brother said to the class that he drinks cola because no church official has ever confirmed that it is against the Word of Wisdom. After the class, someone approached my brother and said that he should not admit that he drinks cola in church in case there are any investigators in attendance.

These petty little incidents used to drive us mad. The Word of Wisdom was more of a health guide when Joseph released it, but in later years, the Church made it a commandment.

I have heard people praising God's foresight regarding smoking. 'In those days people didn't know it was bad for you, but with what we know about it today, you can see how inspired Joseph Smith was'. It is a crying shame that foresight was lacking when black men were denied the priesthood though.

Another part of the Word of Wisdom states that members should eat meat sparingly. In one lesson, someone mentioned this and said all we seem to focus on is not smoking and drinking, but technically, we should also be cutting down our meat intake too. I could see the brethren sweating over this one: no one wanted to sacrifice meat. However, the teacher put everyone's mind at ease, 'No, in those days meat was harder to come by. We live in a world where it is readily available now.' It was this picking and choosing that was confusing for people: do not drink cola, but do not worry about all the junk food you are eating as that is not mentioned in the Word of Wisdom, so it is fine.

The Word of Wisdom was easy enough for me to keep in my teens, as were the Ten Commandments. Yet it was all the other stuff mentioned in a booklet called *For the Strength of Youth*, which I found to be testing. I remember being handed it at church one Sunday and taking it home to read. At first, I thought it was just 'advice', but leaders later told me that I should approach it all as scripture, so that meant doctrine.

Some of it like 'dress and appearance' was a piece of cake for me:

Never lower your standards of dress. Do not use a special occasion as an excuse to be immodest. When you dress immodestly, you send a message that is contrary to your identity as a son or daughter of God. You also send the message that you are using your body to get attention and approval. Immodest clothing is any clothing that is tight, sheer, or revealing in any other manner. Young women should avoid short shorts and short skirts, shirts that do not cover the stomach, and clothing that does not cover the shoulders or is low-cut in the front or the back. Young men should also maintain modesty in their appearance. Young men and young women should be neat and clean and avoid being extreme or inappropriately casual in clothing, hairstyle, and behavior. They should choose appropriately modest apparel when participating in sports. The fashions of the world will change, but the Lord's standards will not change. Do not disfigure yourself with tattoos or body piercings.

Young women, if you desire to have your ears pierced, wear only one pair of earrings.

For the Strength of Youth, pp. 6–7

I was not planning on wearing miniskirts and halter necks, but this was difficult for some of the young women, especially those who lived outside of Utah. The young women would be told: 'As a rule of thumb try and dress as if you were going to be in the Saviour's presence. If you'd feel uncomfortable wearing something in front of Him, then it's probably not appropriate'. As the Lord sent Adam and Eve down in their birthday suits, I am pretty sure He does not care about a cheeky shoulder being on show, not to mention your Christus statue has one of God's nipples showing above the bed sheet you have draped over Him— way to set an example.

I recall some of the young women complaining that it was not particularly easy for them to find shoulder covering or knee length outfits in high street shops. We did not have the internet back then, so they could not order any 'Molly Mormon' attire in either. For boys living in the nineties, this was easy because everything was all about super baggy clothes. I am not sure how today's lads, with their tight shirts and skinny jeans, are handling this though.

I was too young to care about piercings and tattoos as well, so, so far so good. This next one ruined my day though:

Choose carefully the music you listen to. Pay attention to how you feel when you are listening. Some music can carry evil and destructive messages. Do not listen to music that encourages immorality or glorifies violence through its lyrics, beat, or intensity. Do not listen to music that uses vulgar or offensive language or promotes evil practices. Such music can dull your spiritual sensitivity. Learn and sing the hymns. Hymns can lift your spirit, move you to righteous action, and help you withstand the temptations of the adversary.

For the Strength of Youth, p. 22

I was listening to hip hop, rap, punk, grunge, and heavy metal, and the lyrical content included all of the above. There was no way I was going to replace my music with hymns. I ignored this part of the booklet for as long as I could, but every now and then, when I was feeling righteous. I would throw my albums in the trash, then I would re-buy them.

I used to listen to my music at low levels so my parents would not hear the lyrics, and then blast them out when they were not home. When I would feel guilty, I used to try and make tapes that cut out any bad language, or I would just listen to bands that were not as 'parental advisory' as others.

Dancing can be fun and can provide an opportunity to meet new people. However, it too can be misused. When dancing, avoid full body contact with your partner. Do not use positions or moves that are suggestive of sexual or violent behavior or are otherwise inappropriate. Attend only those dances where dress, grooming, lighting, lyrics, music, and entertainment contribute to a wholesome atmosphere where the Spirit may be present.

For the Strength of Youth, p. 23

Was pogoing and crowd-surfing okay? Other than that, I was too polite to start grinding up against girls. At church dances, some adults would keep an eye on the dance floor to make sure the youth were dancing 'a Book of Mormon's length apart'. That was not just a saying. Sometimes, a Book of Mormon was placed between couples who were swaying a little too close together during a slow dance.

The only thing I was not sure about was if the Spirit would be present at a punk rock show. MxPx were Christians, so maybe that could be a compromise.

I had the same concerns with what TV shows or films I was watching. Surely the Spirit would not be up for a movie night if it had any sex or violence in? I was not sure if I could ask Him if he could just close His eyes and cover His ears on certain parts. Probably not, so I guessed we would just have to watch *Star Wars* again.

The Mormon youth loved nothing more than telling each other, 'I went to see (insert film) at the cinema the other day but I walked out and went home because it was inappropriate'. Even when I was fully active at church, I used to think what squares they were. I would never do that after paying for a ticket. I would just pray for forgiveness later that night if the pangs of guilt hit me. Why would an infinite being be so offended by Arnold Schwarzenegger running around a jungle trying to defeat the Predator? That movie was incredible. Is it because of the violence? Does it affect our innocent little elect minds? Okay then, well let me refer you back to one of the first stories in the Book of Mormon. You know the one, Mormons? Where young Nephi hears a voice telling him to obtain the Gold Plates by killing Laban, so Nephi steals the Plates, cuts off Laban's head, and then puts on his bloodstained clothes and pretends to be him to escape the city? Or how about the story where Ammon chops off a group of Lamanites arms and the severed limbs are gathered up into baskets so they can show the king what Ammon did to them?

What about sex in films? I swear that whenever we would have sleepovers at Tim's, the moment boobs came on screen was the moment his mum would walk in the room. There are so many movies we half-watched because we had to turn them off. I guess we should read the Bible instead then? 'Erm, hey Tim, there's a story in here where Lot's daughters get him drunk on wine so that he will shag them, get them both pregnant, and then his posterity can live on'. How is that for an inappropriate sex scene?

'Why though, where has Lot's wife gone?'

'Good question, Tim! God turned her into a pillar of salt four verses ago'. Great foresight, God of the Old Testament, now Lot's wife is dead he had to get his daughters pregnant instead. (Genesis 19:30–36)

Dating

> You should not date until you are at least 16 years old. When you begin dating, go with one or more additional couples. Avoid going on frequent dates with the same person. Developing serious relationships too early in life can limit the number of other people you meet and can perhaps lead to immorality. Invite your parents to become acquainted with those you date. Choose to date only those who have high moral standards and in whose company you can maintain your standards. Remember that a young man and a young woman on a date are responsible to protect each other's honor and virtue.
>
> *For the Strength of Youth*, p. 4

The instruction to 'Avoid going on frequent dates with the same person' was because it 'can perhaps lead to immorality'. Dating was not that straightforward in Britain. We did not just date around like the Utah youth must have been doing. I did not even know many girls well enough to ask them on dates at school. If you liked someone, you became a couple, and you stayed exclusive to each other. I do not remember approaching my first serious relationship with a conversation about protecting each other's honour and virtue either.

I kept hearing the word 'immorality' in church talks and lessons, but I did not exactly know what that meant. I used to think that just meant no sex before marriage. This whole area was a little grey for me.

Warning: I am going to use sex words in this next part, so if you are easily offended then maybe go and put the kettle on and have a hot chocolate if you are a Mormon or a coffee if you are not, and meet back here in a couple of chapters—it is up to you, use your free agency.

Masturbation (I warned you): I learned a little too late in the day that this was a moral sin. I was never taught about this in any of my Sunday school lessons, or from any of my leaders. I never approached my parents about it for obvious reasons, and none of my church friends had ever mentioned it before. I learned about it being a sin when reading a book by the twelfth prophet of the Latter-day Saint church, President Spencer W. Kimball:

Youth come into contact early with masturbation. Many would-be authorities declare that it is natural and acceptable, and frequently young men I interview cite these advocates to justify their practice of it. To this we must respond that the world's norms in many areas—drinking, smoking, and sex experience generally, to mention only a few—depart increasingly from God's law. The Church has a different, higher norm.

Thus prophets anciently and today condemn masturbation. It induces feelings of guilt and shame. It is detrimental to spirituality. It indicates slavery to the flesh, not that mastery of it and the growth toward godhood which is the object of our mortal life. Our modern prophet has indicated that no young man should be called on a mission who is not free from this practice.

While we should not regard this weakness as the heinous sin which some other sexual practices are, it is of itself bad enough to require sincere repentance. What is more, it too often leads to grievous sin, even to that sin against nature, homosexuality. For, done in private, it evolves often into mutual masturbation—practiced with another person of the same sex and thence into total homosexuality.

Spencer W. Kimball, *The Miracle of Forgiveness*, pp. 77-78

I am sure that last paragraph has left you stunned, but I will get back to the subject of homosexuality later. For now, let us get back to me and my penis.

I am pretty sure the Spice Girls got the ball rolling for me—damn that Union Jack dress. After a couple of times, I felt uneasy and then just stopped. I did not really think about it much until I got a girlfriend. After a while, we moved on from kissing to foreplay, or 'heavy petting', as the Church calls it. All I knew for sure back then was that I was not allowed to have sex, but the other stuff was okay, was it not? I did not know that it was not okay for months. I even asked a couple of my older church friends what the rules are and they told me the following:

'You can't have sex, but you can do everything else. It's risky though because the other stuff can lead to sex. It's like getting into the sea with a shark. The shark is sex, so you want to avoid it, but you can enjoy swimming, but it's still dangerous'.

I was a little confused, but they made me feel better about what I had been up to. I also trusted that they knew more about it all than me as they were a couple of years older than I was. It was not until I read *The Miracle of Forgiveness* that I realised that I had been sinning. I also began to notice scriptures which spoke about sexual sin more than I had before. The Book of Mormon, Alma: 39:5, says:

Know ye not, my son, that these things are an abomination in the sight of the Lord; yea, most abominable above all sins save it be the shedding of innocent blood or denying the Holy Ghost?

I could not believe how serious it was—sexual sin sat just below murder and apostasy in God's eyes. I began to worry. In my ignorance, I had really messed up, and so I talked to my dad about it all. Dad was pretty chilled out about it and made the conversation easier than I expected. He advised me to speak with our bishop about it too because he could help me repent.

As I sat across from the bishop to confess my sins for the very first time, I handed over my spiritual freedom and became incarcerated in a private hell that would last for years.

8

Guilt

There are some sins that you can repent of yourself, but sexual sins must be confessed to your bishop.

In a nutshell, the repentance process is as follows: you feel sorrow for what you have done; make restitution where possible; pray for forgiveness; and then change your behaviour so that you do not repeat the transgression. Taking the sacrament on a Sunday is a way for members to renew their covenants with God too.

I have been in a lot of confession sessions with several bishops over the years so it is difficult to differentiate them all now. What I will never forget though is the sense of shame, unworthiness, embarrassment, and humiliation I felt as I sat at the bishop's desk, discussing my immorality. One memory that does stand out though is when one bishop told me to imagine the nails being smashed into Christ's hands as a pleasant little aid to help me concentrate on staying worthy.

Some bishops did not care for going into any details of my transgressions. 'Heavy petting' or 'masturbation' was sufficient enough for them to understand what sin I was repenting. It was always awkward and degrading and in later life, I realised that it never made me feel any better. I used to think that it did, but all it actually achieved was confirm that I was impure. I would be told not to partake of the sacrament for a few weeks because I was not worthy. I was not worthy to pass or bless the sacrament either, which was hard to be discreet about.

'Hey Chris, can you bless the sacrament with me?'

'Sorry mate, I can't.' It did not go unnoticed when the sacrament would be passed to me, and my family would just see me pass the tray along without partaking of the bread or water.

In later years, I learned that most of my friends rarely went to confess to a bishop. I always did because I was constantly wracked with terrible guilt for my sins and I believed that if I did not confess, then I would not be forgiven. If I was not forgiven then the Spirit would not be with me. If the Spirit was not with me then I lost all confidence in myself as a person. I relied heavily on having the Holy Ghost as a companion, to protect me, to guide me, to inspire me, and to uplift me. When that was gone, I was a wreck.

I was terrified of not being spiritually worthy. I was constantly being told that the Second Coming of Christ was probably going to happen in my lifetime. Many of the biblical prophecies were being fulfilled. There were wars and rumours of wars. There were earthquakes and floods. The gospel was spreading into every land. The world was becoming more wicked and we were the elect generation reserved for this very moment in time to usher in the arrival of Christ. At any moment, the sky could tear apart and Christ could appear. What if I was unclean? How ashamed would I be? I would feel devastated if I was not ready for Him. From time to time, I had apocalyptic nightmares about the Second Coming and being ill-prepared for it. I wanted to make sure I was worthy to meet the Saviour of the world with clean hands, but it was not that simple.

When I was sixteen, I would be resisting all of the natural teenage urges for weeks and weeks, until eventually, I would 'slip' (as I used to call it). Whether it was on my own or with my girlfriend, I would instantly feel regret. I would go to bed, bunch up in a ball, and cry out to God.

'Father in Heaven, I'm so sorry. I've messed up again. Please forgive me. I know I'm unworthy before you, but please don't take away your Spirit. Please don't leave me! I know your Son died for me. I'm sorry that I caused Him pain. I feel so ashamed of myself. I'll try harder next time. I promise you that I will change, just please forgive me and send the Spirit back to me. Please give me the strength to resist temptation. Please apply the Atonement to me. In the name of Jesus Christ, I plead, Amen.' I would lay there feeling empty and forsaken until I would eventually fall asleep.

A prayer like this would be repeated all week, until I saw the bishop and confessed. Then, I knew mentally that I had done all that was required to repent. I do not think a bishop ever uplifted me and made me feel any better; I used to just do it because I knew I had to in order to obtain forgiveness.

I would try and change my ways. I would read more scriptures and try not to be alone with my girlfriend if I could, but I was weak. I was young and knee-deep in teenage romance. I wanted to be with her but I knew that I could not. I knew that I could still serve a mission in three more years if I did not go all the way, so that really kept me from full blown sexual intercourse. I would always mess up though with other stuff and the whole process would be repeated.

Sometimes, I would feel spiritually exhausted and go numb. During these brief periods, I was passed caring anymore and I accepted my weakness. I would carry on sinning and ignoring the guilt that was always tapping on my shoulder. This almost felt better than being a broken mess, but it never lasted long. I would go to church, hear a talk that would humble me, and I would be raking myself through the fiery coals again.

It was also terrifying for me if I had slipped up and was then asked to give a talk at church, or teach a lesson, or give someone a priesthood blessing. I knew the Spirit was not with me, so how could I possibly do any of those things? My confidence would be shot to bits. I needed the Spirit to function.

I would pray through it. 'Dear Lord, I know that I am unworthy, but please forgive me, please let me be inspired anyway so that I can at least help others. Please let your Spirit bless others even though this vessel is unclean'. When I reflect, I am appalled by the words I used to describe myself—I was sixteen and branding myself 'unclean, unworthy, impure, immoral, and weak'.

Most guys my age were going to bed thinking about girls they liked, while I was soaking my pillows with tears as I begged for mercy. I feared that I was never going to make it to heaven and I was never going to be with my family and friends in the next life. It would be a miracle if I could get myself out on a mission.

A letter I wrote to my dad reminded me of how I felt:

Dear Dad,

I woke up this morning and decided to write to you. It really is difficult to explain. I'm not sure where to start because it's all feelings. I just feel down. In three months I should be getting the Melchizedek Priesthood. Dad, I haven't even honoured the Aaronic Priesthood I have now. Am I ready for the higher priesthood and does Heavenly Father want me to have it? I do not know where I stand with Heavenly Father anymore. I feel that all my sins still rest on my back. Every time I am tempted or thoughts come to me, I am reminded of my awful state. I can't escape it.

I am going to serve a mission, but I'm not looking forward to the day that I have to say goodbye to my family and Laura. I can't bear the thought. I only have fifteen months to sort my life out. One of the most important things to do is make sure I feel forgiven, and prepare spiritually.

It's hard to explain my feelings, Dad. I haven't done a very good job. The last time I confessed my sins to the bishop, it was a strange experience. I met with him two times and he didn't talk about it at all. He asked me two questions and that was it. It was like he was fed up with the same old story. He looked disappointed. I feel like the black sheep of the ward.

I feel low and I can't lift myself. I just hope Heavenly Father will forgive me of my sins. I'm sorry for all I do wrong. I love you all very much, and I'm proud to be in this family. I just feel ashamed and guilty.

I'm grateful for all you have done. You've always shown me light when I saw nothing but darkness. Thanks.

Love,
Chris

I finished school and started college, but I continued to be tormented by temptation and sin.

I must have been such an asshole of a boyfriend. Whenever we got intimate, I would immediately be overcome with guilt and show my regret. On one occasion,

I knew that a youth activity was being held nearby my house, so literally after the moment we finished, I got up, dressed, left my girlfriend half-naked on the bed, and went to the youth activity to confess to the bishop. I feel sorry for doing that now, but at the time, my mind was so brainwashed that I could not bear the thought of going another five days plagued by guilt. I could not wait for Sunday; I needed it immediately resolved. I ran over to the bishop and asked if I could speak with him. He could tell I was distressed and so he ended up taking me to his home to talk about it. I spent a long time in his home office talking with him, and I ended up sleeping on his sofa for the night. Soon after this, I broke up with my girlfriend of two years.

This particular bishop was a really great guy. I looked up to him and I respected him. He did not make me feel like previous bishops had. For once, I was receiving wise counsel and he helped me understand that I needed to prepare properly for my mission. I could not afford any distractions anymore. I was never going to break the cycle, so I needed change. Both my dad and the bishop supported me and helped me realise that I had to remove temptation from my life. It hurt me a lot to end the relationship and I was upset, even a bit shell-shocked, for quite a while, but I knew that I had to get myself right with the Lord and serve a mission. For the first time in years, I felt a massive weight lift from my shoulders. My spiritual cleansing had begun.

9

The Phoney War

Tuesday, 19 September 2000.

Today I am going to wage war against Satan and his demons. I am going to use prayer, fasting, the scriptures, my family, friends, and leaders. Most importantly my Saviour Jesus Christ. Last night a friend lent me a talk tape called *The Difference One Can Make*. It's by Larry Johnson (not the NBA star) and he talks about a seminary student he loved called Kent Williams. This has inspired me to make a fresh start and to try and be better than I ever have. To be worthy, pure, clean, righteous, a good example, polite, friendly, and loving. Maybe the word 'charity' sums it up. I want to be more like the Lord; I desire to improve my life. Kent Williams, although I have never met him sounds like a great young man. I want to be this kind of man. He was killed three weeks into his mission by a train. The tape spoke about his journal entries and they are inspiring. I have been motivated by this tape and I want to be better than I ever have been. It starts today. I serve a mission shortly and I want to be ready and prepared. I am going to stay close to my Heavenly Father in prayer; I will read the scriptures daily and serve others. I am going to overcome Satan. I know it will take me a very long time but eventually I will do it because I have faith in Christ. 'I can do all things through Christ which strengtheneth me'. I would like to start by sharing my testimony, I know without any doubt that The Church of Jesus Christ of Latter-day Saints is the only true church upon the earth today. I have a loving Heavenly Father who watches me every day, who looks after me, and wants me to be happy. He has a son, Jesus Christ, my Lord and Saviour, my King. He is my older brother. He died for me upon the cross, He atones for my sins, and He suffered so much pain because He loves me. He has shown me so much mercy and love in my life; He has forgiven me of my sins. He has given me the opportunity to return home to the Kingdom of Heaven. I am so thankful for the love the Holy Ghost has put into my heart, the peace, and inexpressible joy. I love my family so much. I am blessed with goodly parents and a great brother. I love the scriptures and I am so thankful for them. They have the fullness of the gospel and they bring great comfort to me.

That seems like a classic eighteen-year-old journal entry, does it not? Did anyone else get home from college and declare war against the Devil and the hosts of Hell in their spare time?

I felt confident that I could defeat them. Sure, I was trapped in the body that God gave me, which turned out to be a natural enemy to my spirit, but that was just details. I was going to *blitzkrieg* my way through evil and triumph victorious so that one day I would be accepted into Heaven.

I rediscovered this journal when I was thirty-five years old and I cringed at first. I then laughed as I read it aloud to my wife, but privately I was overcome with sadness. It was heart-breaking to remember how deluded I was, and possibly mentally ill. I remember this period well, because it was what I considered to be the most righteous time of my church life.

When I turned eighteen, I was given the Melchizedek priesthood, also known as the higher priesthood. This gave me more responsibility as a young man. At the time, I found this to be a great honour and a privilege, despite being told that I would be held accountable in the next life if I did not receive it, and that 'whoso breaketh this covenant after he hath received it, and altogether turneth therefrom, shall not have forgiveness of sins in this world nor in the world to come' (Doctrine and Covenants 84:81)—'damned if I do, damned if I don't'. 'Damn it,' I thought, 'I am officially damned.'

My new responsibilities meant that I was able to have my very own home teaching list rather than be a junior companion, and more importantly, I was now able to give blessings to people.

In the Church, the priesthood is given to people by the laying on of hands by someone with the correct priesthood authority. My dad held the Melchizedek priesthood and so he gave it to me when I became of age. If you have no idea what I am talking about then this is what happened:

I sat on a chair and closed my eyes. My dad placed his hands on my head and closed his eyes. Whoever I wanted to assist in the blessing (priesthood holders) laid their hands on my head and closed their eyes too. My dad would then say the required words to confer the priesthood upon me and then freestyle. Well, I say freestyle, but the Church will say that it is 'speaking as the Spirit dictates'.

When you have the higher priesthood, you can also bless the sick or give blessings of comfort to people who ask for them. I did this a lot when I was eighteen. The very first blessing I ever gave was to my bishop—no pressure there then. I forget the exact reason for the blessing now, but it was either that he wanted to change jobs or go for a promotion and so he asked me to give him a blessing to help him be guided and to achieve this. I am pretty sure he also wanted to throw me in the deep end and for me to get experience. I was so nervous, but I gave the blessing to the best of my ability.

Giving a blessing is a strange process. You have to get into a particular headspace to allow yourself to be guided by the Spirit. Beforehand, I would pray, read my scriptures, and maybe even fast to make sure that I was 'in tune' with the Spirit.

When the time came to administer the blessing, I would begin by saying the required words and then pause for a moment. Then, it was time to freestyle. As I had prayed earlier and done my best to be in tune, I would have faith that whatever I was saying was guided by the Spirit and trust that God would honour the blessing through the priesthood authority.

If you are receiving a blessing, the experience can be comforting and uplifting. A priesthood blessing creates an atmosphere of seriousness and reverence. You are feeling needy and you know you are being blessed by someone with the authority to do it—not even the Queen can do this. So, whatever is said you receive it as gospel.

When I was Mormon, I used to believe that blessings worked because I would usually see people uplifted or comforted by the practice. I would also feel empowered because the Lord had deemed me worthy enough to speak on His behalf; now, I believe that the whole process is just an illusion.

You have physical contact with someone when you are gently laying your hands on their head. This creates trust and intimacy. I believe the freestyling element to a blessing is also just positive affirmations being said which convinces both parties that the Spirit is present. When you are being blessed with what you want to hear then of course you are going to feel better.

Here is a journal entry I made after giving a blessing, which will give you a better insight into the whole experience:

Tonight James and I went out to give a Sister a blessing as she is unwell. James anointed (a drop of blessed Olive oil was placed onto the crown of the head) and I blessed. After we went tracting and gave out a few leaflets and spoke to a few people. After we went to Gerald's home in hope of uplifting him and inviting him back out to church. We talked with him for a while and then James and I shared some scriptures with him and invited him to turn to the Lord with his problems. Before we left he asked for a priesthood blessing. James anointed and I sealed it. I cannot find the words to express this experience. The Spirit filled me and I spoke the words of the Lord, or what the Lord put into my heart. It was wonderful, a very powerful blessing. Gerald was in tears and so was James. I felt very humbled. The Lord spoke directly to Gerald; he poured out his Spirit upon him and filled him with so much love and peace. After the blessing Gerald hugged me and just cried. The Spirit was so strong. We knelt in prayer and Gerald prayed to the Lord after he thanked us. His whole countenance changed, he seemed so much happier and alive. I felt how much Jesus Christ and Heavenly Father loved him and it bore testimony to me of the Lord's love for His People, His family.

... I feel the blessing helped us all. It uplifted Gerald and gave him love and motivation, and taught James and I the power the Lord has to change our lives, in the very moment. I am blessed with the authority to hold the priesthood, blessed with the opportunity to serve and to minister to others and in this I praise the Lord my God.

Sometimes, a Mormon friend will ask me to remember my past 'spiritual' experiences in an attempt to reignite my faith, but when I read these experiences again over a decade later, I just feel cold. My language back then repulses me and it just reminds me that I had lost my mind to Mormon delusion.

Gerald was uplifted because two friends had taken the time to come and see how he was doing. All three of us were under the same spell, so the experience was what we all needed it to be. We had cherry-picked faith-promoting scriptures out for him, the only kind he had been hoping to hear. I have no idea what I said that day but the blessing was likely filled with all kinds of positive affirmations, which temporarily dispelled his blues. Even praying together creates a bond between people.

I am sure Mormons will say that I am being too cynical about this experience now that I have denied the truth of what happened, but I cannot trick myself into a false sense of spiritual security anymore.

Since the outbreak of war in September, I had not seen any combat with the enemy. I was wondering if the Devil had retreated since I was ordained to the Melchizedek priesthood. Leaders kept telling me that the adversary will strike soon though because he did not want me to serve a mission. They were right. When I submitted my mission application papers, the phoney war was over.

My papers have been in a little over a week now. I have felt the Adversary trying to pull me down at times, in different areas of my life. I've been feeling very tired, stressed out, and ill. He has also been trying to get at my thoughts. I must confess I have had impure thoughts that I ought not to have, and Satan has attempted to tempt me with immorality. I write this because I want to record how Satan tries to stop young people from going on missions.

It has been about five months now since Laura and I finished. In that time I have not had any contact with her at all. In the last couple of weeks I have seen her twice, not to talk to, but just seen in passing. I write this because it caused a few strange feelings inside of me. Once again I outline how Satan tries anything that could stop a preparing missionary.

I just wish that I had followed the Lord's council of not dating outside of the Church, it does not work, but I leave all of my mistakes in the past.

I have overcome these things. I have not given way to these temptations because I have prayed, prayed that I may have strength and read my scriptures. These two key elements have helped me in these things.

... I, with all my heart, want to be a missionary.

In hindsight, I feel sheepish about my attitude back then. Laura was an awesome person, my first love even, and my immaturity and selfishness prevented us from remaining friends.

As I prepared for a mission, I went into spiritual overdrive. If you knew me during this time then the chances are you were given a copy of the Book of Mormon with my testimony written in the front. I gave one to everyone I came across. My work colleagues, my school friends, and my college friends all got the Book of Mormon dropped into their hands whether they liked it or not.

When I was not at college or working, I would spend my time knocking on doors with my friend James. We gave out tons of church pamphlets and dozens of Books of Mormon in our local area. We taught some people about the First Vision and set up appointments for the missionaries. One person we talked with even came out to church. The missionaries in our ward appreciated the help, and the bishop would often call us out in church meetings as being good examples of member missionaries.

I remember thinking we had found our 'golden' investigator on one occasion. He opened the door and listened to our pitch, and then told us that he had been receiving visits from an angel—holy miracles, Batman. We have been sent here for a reason. When we inquired further, our hopes soon evaporated.

'Yeah, every night Bill Shankly appears to me, and we discuss the Liverpool squad. I pray to him every night.' I thought he was joking at first, but he was nuts.

I felt really in tune with God during this time. I knew that I was doing all that I could, and more, to serve Him and to practice what I preached. I was ploughing my way through the scriptures and church literature. I would listen to church talk tapes and accompany missionaries while they taught people. I would stay up at all hours talking about spiritual subjects with my friends. I was even helping other home teaching pairs make their monthly visits. I got so high and mighty that I even cut out music and TV from my life for a while to focus on my studies and to draw closer to Christ. My inappropriate films and CDs ended up in the bin too; my dad found them and took them out because he knew I would want them back again at some point.

Even at college, I was preaching. Towards the end of my course, we were assigned to give a presentation to the class on any subject we wanted so that we could complete our communications skills. I spent weeks preparing my presentation. I was going to talk about the greatest basketball player of all time, Michael Jordan. I researched his life story, I printed out visual aids, and I had video footage on hand.

The night before my presentation I was reading the scriptures and I suddenly felt inspired to change my topic. I believed that the Lord was telling me to talk about Joseph Smith and the Church instead. At first, I winced because this was going to be quite hard for me to do. As much as I was proud of my religion,

I had not really announced it to the rest of my class or to my teachers. Most of them were not really 'religious' types either. They were all too busy enjoying experiences that I was repressing. I tried to ignore the 'prompt', but then I started to feel guilty about my disobedience. 'Are you ashamed of me?' Of course not. 'Well then.' Once guilt seeped into my system, I was done for. I disregarded my M. J. presentation and decided that I would teach the First Vision instead.

I felt so sick in class that day, but I got up and did it anyway. I spoke about Joseph Smith and his vision, I presented them with the Book of Mormon, and I told them that once I had finished college, I would be going on a mission. 'I could end up in Africa or even Japan'. It felt awkward to be talking about the gospel in the cold light of day at college, but I felt relieved when it was over. I had done what the Lord had asked of me, and that feeling was like a drug to me. When class finished everyone had a question ready. The lads were fascinated that I was not allowed to have sex or jerk off.

One of my friends was joining the Commandos after college. He said to me, 'At least me and you are doing something exciting with our lives and not just going to uni'.

I did not convert any of them, but I did appreciate how they made me feel cool about my peculiar presentation. Maybe there are good non-Mormons in the world?

After I had received the all-clear from my doctor, once he ran some tests and held my nuts, I was deemed fit to serve a mission. I sent my papers off and endured a long wait for my call to come through. My journal entries are full of frustration and impatience, and I always seemed to be ill. I was showing signs of anxiety about where I would be called and I was worried about leaving my friends and family. This was all natural though. My resolve was always longing to be a missionary.

It seemed all I did was work at my boring job in a video store and think about the Church. Surprisingly though, I did go to a punk rock show with a college friend, and like a true dork, I recorded this in my journal: 'Last night I saw MxPx play at the London Astoria. They were great, and didn't swear once! … I went with Tom, and gave him a Book of Mormon and a leaflet with Joseph Smith's testimony in it.'

On 14 November 2000, Mum woke me up to tell me that my mission call has arrived in the post. It read:

Dear Elder Yeoman,

　　You are hereby called to serve as a missionary of The Church of Jesus Christ of Latter-day Saints. You are assigned to labor in the California Roseville Mission. It is anticipated that you will serve for a period of 24 months.

　　You should report to the Missionary Training Centre at Provo, Utah, on Wednesday, 10th January 2001. You will prepare to preach the gospel in the English language.

The letter was signed by President Gordon B. Hinckley, who was the current prophet of the Church. No matter how I feel about the Church today, I still have a tremendous amount of respect for Gordon B.; whether I believe he was a prophet or not is irrelevant as he seemed like a kind, lovely gent to me. After such a long wait for my call to arrive, I was thrilled:

> I'm so happy, so blessed! My prayers have been answered more than I possibly imagined. I think we have phoned everyone now. My family are so excited too.
> ... It's cool, we've been looking up California on our maps and we have marked Roseville.

It was great to be home for Christmas as well. I was sure that I was going to leave before December, but the delay of my call coming through had worked out for the best. It was the worst Christmas though as far as gifts were concerned: shirts, ties, and suits for my mission. 'Surprise! Another white shirt!'

Everyone at my local church and neighbouring wards rallied around me, except one lady who my dad heard ask, 'Why is my son not going on a mission, but someone from the Yeoman family is?' Apart from Sister 'Sourpuss', I was getting a lot of support and encouragement. So many people were generous in helping me acquire everything I would need for a mission. Several less-active members also donated money and bought me clothes. I was overwhelmed by everyone's kindness and excitement. The leaders were proud of me and I knew that I was finally clean, worthy, and ready.

Before my mission, I was required to go through the Temple to receive my endowments and to make new covenants with God. I was washed and anointed, a ritual that symbolised my purification before God and taught the signs and tokens I would need in order to be able to enter the Kingdom of Heaven. The Temple ceremony was not like I had imagined. I did not expect to learn secret handshakes and to chant with a silly hat on my head, but I got through it without much trouble and like a good little Mormon I accepted it as the Lord's way.

One of these new temple covenants required me to wear sacred garments, which took some getting used to. Someone close to me refers to them as 'passion killers' because they are not the most flattering underwear in the world. There was one awkward night for me when I went back to a girl's place and forgot that I was wearing them, but that is a story for another time.

Mormons believe temple garments to be a sacred subject, but garments have been exposed all over the internet already and have even appeared in a couple of well-known TV shows. I am not being disrespectful by mentioning them, if anything, I am doing Mormonism a favour when I say that they are not 'magic underpants', as some people like to call them. There is nothing magical about them. They are sacred reminders of your temple covenants and they are supposed to offer spiritual protection. Of course, there are always mythological stories about how they have protected people from physical injuries, but I never really bought into that. One guy told me he fell of a building and bounced off a metal pole because he was wearing his garments. I have also heard tales about soldiers being protected from bullets, but I have never taken them seriously. There are tons of urban legends in the Church. None of them are official, but the stories have a way of circulating. The worst one I heard was about two missionaries being too lazy to turn the light off when they were already in bed (not together, or maybe they were), so they tried to use the priesthood to turn the light switch off, like some bad Jedi force trick. Apparently, they were found dead the next morning. I never believed this nonsense; someone had probably made this up as a cautionary tale about using the priesthood inappropriately, though if I die before this book has been published, someone will say it is because I was apostatising.

Me and my parents at my missionary farewell gathering, 2001

10

The Haze

The South African missionary that converted my parents flew over to the UK with his family two weeks before I was due to leave for the States. They lived in Utah, so I was able to fly back to their home with them the night before I was due to enter the Missionary Training Centre (MTC) in Provo. It was great to finally meet Mark. The last time he saw me was when I was a toddler. My parents were thrilled about the reunion as well. We spent two brilliant weeks together as families before my departure.

The farewell at the airport was really tough for me and my family. After a lot of hugs and tears, I stepped onto an aircraft for the first time in my life.
Mark's family and I flew to Atlanta and then boarded a plane to Salt Lake City, Utah. I recall being really tired when we arrived. It was dark and cold and the city seemed like an alien world compared to London. Despite the temperature, it was breath-taking to be surrounded by large snow-capped mountains. There appeared to be Mormon statues, chapels, and temples everywhere I looked. This was the Mormon capital of the world after all.

We arrived at Mark's house in Orem, Utah, and I phoned my family to let them know that I was safe and to say our final goodbyes. From then on, I would only be allowed to communicate with my family by writing letters once a week.

I need to be up front with you here. Most of my mission experience is very hazy to me now, so I apologise for this part of the book not being as detailed as I would have liked. When I returned home, I destroyed all of my mission journals, so I have not been able to reference them. I remember the broad strokes and my emotions, but that is it.

I spent some of the night talking to one of Mark's daughters, Kira. She was a sweet girl and helped me feel at ease in my new surroundings. She gave me a photo of her to take with me. I felt like a Second World War soldier leaving for Normandy.

The next day, Mark and Kira dropped me off at the MTC. I remember listening to a talk (probably by the MTC president) and then saying goodbye to Mark and Kira. A lot of missionaries had their families with them and it was an emotional atmosphere. I wished that my family could have been there too.

Saying goodbye to my brother, David, with a hug at the airport. His expression says it all.

Me as a missionary in Provo, Utah, 2001.

In the MTC, I was assigned a missionary companion called Elder Travis. When we become missionaries, we all have the title of 'elder' and then our surnames. Elder Travis was from Utah and he seemed like a fun guy. We shared a room with two other missionaries—one was from Chicago and I think the other was also from Utah. My English accent soon drew attention and a lot of the missionaries sharing nearby rooms wanted to talk with me. Some of them were genuinely shocked that we had the internet in the UK, and that we were not still living under the great smog of London. Our rooms were pretty basic and dull. They reminded me of eighties army barracks or prison cells. I had a desk and a bottom bunk bed and that was about it.

Every morning, we would wake up at about 5.30 a.m. or 6 a.m. to get showered and dressed in time for a day of classes. I was not too pleased about the showering arrangements. We had what Provo attendees called 'tree of life' showers: one vertical plumbing unit with six shower heads attached. This meant that on my first morning in the MTC, I was standing in a naked circle with five other strange dudes. It was terribly awkward, made even more so when some rookie let a bar of soap slip out of his fingers and onto the floor. I could not help myself. 'Come on mate, you know what happens if you drop the soap'. I chuckled to myself and looked up at five blank expressions. Not one of them even cracked a half-smile. I guess prison humour was wasted on these guys. I was here for three weeks, so I decided that I would get up as early as I was able to avoid a crowded shower in the morning. Seeing a bunch of dicks at the butt crack of dawn was not how I wanted to start my day.

The urban legends began to spread quickly in Provo. 'This one guy ran out of the MTC and was hit by a truck and died. Another time this guy was so delirious with trying to escape from the MTC that he started climbing up the mountains and fell off'.

Another highlight was that I was soon told by my companion that he was having masturbation problems and so he had been confessing to the MTC president. I thought, 'Are you bloody serious? You've only been here a week so far and there is nothing here to make you feel aroused. This place makes my manhood invert. There is nothing here but beige walls and paintings of Christ.'

My hard-fought righteous prepared self was disappointed with him. This was not what I wanted in a companion. I wanted someone who was on the same page as me, but he kept talking about Britney Spears and all the girls he used to date. Our companionship studies were dire too. I wondered why he had even bothered to come on a mission.

I soon bonded with a Canadian missionary called Elder Kent who I shared classes with. He was a really cool, down to earth guy and I instantly got along with him. We would hang out together whenever we could and we spent a lot of time getting to know each other. He liked the same bands as I did, he had been through relationship struggles before his mission like I had, and he was really trying to be a diligent missionary. I think we also bonded because we were not from Utah like most of our comrades. Most of the Utah crew seemed so sheltered and naïve to me; I wondered if the cold Utah air had frozen their brains. One day in class, I heard a few of them talking about the reason for them not feeling the Spirit in the MTC, and they concluded that because they lived in Utah, they had become immune to it. They were just so used to living in God's chosen State that they could not recognise it anymore. Maybe these chaps were the elect of the elect? Apparently, the Spirit ran through their veins. Actually, they were mostly on missions so that their families did not disown them and so that Mormon girls would date them in two years. I am not being harsh—I heard some of them say as much.

A typical day in the MTC was personal scripture study and prayer, companionship study and prayer, and then a long day of classes. It is all a blur to me now. I only remember one teacher and that is only because he was a hard-arse. He was strict and arrogant and I did not like him all that much. I too was not feeling the Spirit in Utah, and it was not because I was immune to it.

I had always preached the gospel from my heart or from the scriptures, but at the MTC, I was being taught the skills of a salesman. There was not any flexibility either; you had to teach it by the script not the Spirit. The only thing that was your own was when bearing testimony, but again, all of our testimony mantras sounded the same. What I hated most about missionary training was being asked to bear your testimony in class on the spot. I always thought you should bear testimony when you felt prompted to do it. When a teacher would call on someone in class to stand up and bear testimony, it went down like a cup of cold sick. Another odd thing to be doing was teaching each other about Joseph Smith and the First Vision like no one in the room had heard it before. I remember seeing one guy really struggling to preach to the converted and he just burst into tears. We were constantly tired and unenthusiastic. It was worse than being at school.

I felt let down. I had been preparing for this for so long but it was not anything like I had imagined it to be. I had been led to believe that we would all be having an incredible spiritual journey in Provo. I thought the Spirit would be so tangible and inspiring, but I felt empty. I did not feel anything in the MTC, nor in the Provo Temple. I had never felt so far away from Christ.

It felt strange being disconnected from God and my family. I knew my parents and my brother were upset to see me leave but they were doing their best to put on brave faces. It must have been hard for them to adjust to my mission too.

While I was in the MTC, I received this letter from my brother:

Hi Chris,

How is the MTC? I'm finding it really hard without you. I can't sleep on my own and I am finding it really hard to walk into my own bedroom without you there. You'll be pleased to know that I'm leaving all your Buffy posters on the walls.

In my MTC room, studying the scriptures.

Chris, you will be the best missionary that has ever served in Roseville. Leaving you at the airport was the hardest thing I have ever had to do, but don't worry about us, we will be fine.

What is your new companion like? Be honest!

We will always be praying for you and I promise that all the things you told us to do, we are doing.

You are my best friend and I love you tons. If you be yourself on your mission, many families will love you and you will touch many lives. Keep doing what's right and the Lord will bless you.

Love,

David.

Can I just take a moment to remind you all that we were on missions voluntarily, unpaid, and giving up two years of our lives to serve the Church? Yes, one prophet had declared that it is a commandment that 'every young man should serve a mission', but were we not owed a tiny amount of gratitude or respect?

One afternoon, I was walking through the MTC when a leader pulled me to one side and chastised me for wearing a tiny pin-badge on my suit, which bore the Union Jack and the American flag. 'Elder, that badge detracts from the message, get it off!' I felt so small and it did not make any sense. By that logic,

Walking through the Missionary Training Centre, Provo, Utah, 2001.

then surely my accent would also announce that I am a Brit in America, so does that 'detract from the message too', you arrogant prick?

I was nineteen and so far from home and from people that I could relate to. My letters from my family and friends were so slow to arrive that I began to feel a little isolated. I do not remember a single leader or teacher boosting me up or making me feel welcome to be there. To make matters worse, someone had sneaked in a radio and found out that Jason Newsted had left Metallica.

On our 'day off' to do laundry and exercise, we did not have to wear our suits. In the afternoon, I was headed to the basketball court but I was stopped by a couple of missionaries who chastised me for wearing a Green Day hoodie that my brother had given to me as a gift before I left. I was told that it was inappropriate and I should not be wearing it here. There was nothing inappropriate on it; it was just because they were offended by the band's lyrics.

The overriding message that was drilled into us daily in the MTC was the need to be obedient: obedience, obedience, obedience. It is the only message I actually remember with any clarity. We had to be obedient to mission rules or else the Spirit would withdraw from us and we could not teach with the Holy Ghost as a companion.

There is a little white book we were given called the *Missionary Handbook*. Much like *For the Strength of Youth*, it contained the rules we were required to live by. We were told many times over that these rules were to be taken as seriously as commandments. Here is an example of how militant and specific this book is:

Hair. Keep your hair relatively short (not clipped too close) and evenly tapered. Extreme or faddish styles— including spiked, permed, or bleached hair or a shaved head—are not appropriate. Sideburns should reach no lower than the middle of the ear. (See the pictures of a missionary haircut included with your call packet.) Elders should shave each day.

Missionary Handbook, p. 11.

I had the tiniest spiked fringe at the time and in front of the class, a teacher instructed me to comb it over to one side.

Thank God for Elder Kent—he was my lifeline in the MTC. I do not know how I would have gotten through it without him. At the end of the third week, some of our roommates began to leave for their missions. I think we were due to leave the day after, so we all stayed up and made the most of our final moments together. I was sorry to see some of them go, but we all made false promises to stay in touch, so it was not too bad. Elder Kent and I stayed up chatting in a corridor until 5 a.m. I knew that we would actually keep in touch when we separated, and we have, even to this day.

My MTC class outside of the Provo Temple, 2001.

11

Roseville, CA

Those of us heading to the Roseville, California mission got on a plane and flew to Sacramento. I do not remember much about the trip other than us all being excited to finally be free from the MTC. Utah was cold and the air caused my nose to bleed quite often. I remember feeling free up in the air as we flew over Lake Tahoe. I was glad to still be with Elder Kent for a little while longer.

The next memory I have is being in a room, perhaps in a chapel somewhere, and being told that my new companion was a missionary called Elder Taylor. He was an experienced missionary in Roseville, and he would be showing me the ropes. Elder Taylor was a friendly lad from Utah who loved to smile and laugh. I was instantly relieved that he was going to be my trainer. I said goodbye to Elder Kent, and my mission had officially begun.

Elder Taylor and I lived in an annex on one of the local member's property, in a posh gated community called Granite Bay. We had our own room above a garage with a small kitchen space and bathroom downstairs. I remember stocking up on cola as soon as I got there. I had spent three weeks drinking non-caffeinated drinks in the MTC, and was desperate for a taste of the good stuff. I was also testing my companion to see how he would react. I was pleased to discover that he was not a Word of Wisdom Nazi. I liked this guy already.

I remember my first evening appointment in Granite Bay because I was required to teach a Mormon family the 'first discussion'. As expected, it was forced and weird bearing my testimony about things they already had a testimony of. I felt so green, but I knew my scriptures well and I knew that I would be a good missionary when I got into the flow of things. I decided to be more flexible in the way I presented the gospel too. Rather than depend on the MTC salesman pitches, I would teach from the heart. My companion was an honest, by-the-heart type too, so our approach was very similar, and we worked well together.

I was feeling so tired for our second appointment that night. I just remember eating salad in a member's kitchen and mumbling answers to their questions about England.

My useless bike I had to ride around in Roseville, California, 2001.

In my nervous exhaustion, I had forgotten to collect a bike from the airport that Mark had given me to use on my mission, so I was given a really old, bust-up bike to ride around on instead. The chain would always fall off and I was not used to riding alongside five lanes of traffic. I was shattered before I even arrived at our appointments.

During my first week, we generally visited local Mormon families for me to practice on, but we also spent timing knocking on doors and speaking to people we came across. My accent drew a lot of attention, which helped us to engage in conversations with people. I was really worried about it detracting from the message though.

A typical day in the life of a missionary was as follows:

6.30 a.m. Arise, pray, exercise (thirty minutes), and prepare for the day.

7.30 a.m. Breakfast.

8 a.m. Personal study: the Book of Mormon, other scriptures, missionary library, and Preach My Gospel. Emphasize the doctrines of the missionary lessons.

9 a.m. Companion study: share what you have learned during personal study, prepare to teach, practice teaching, study chapters from Preach My Gospel, and confirm plans for the day.

10 a.m. Begin proselyting (or language study for thirty to sixty minutes). You may take an hour for lunch and additional study and an hour for dinner at

times during the day that fit best with your proselyting time. Normally, dinner should be finished no later than 6 p.m.

Return to living quarters (unless teaching a lesson; then return by 9.30 p.m.), and plan the next day's activities (thirty minutes). Write in your journal, prepare for bed, pray.

10.30 p.m. Retire to bed.

Missionary Handbook, pp. 14–15.

I assumed that we were to use our own initiative if we needed to pee. The worst part of the missionary commandments for me was this one:

COMMUNICATING WITH FAMILY Write to your family each week on preparation day. Limit correspondence with others. Share your spiritual experiences. Never include anything confidential, sensitive, or negative about the areas where you serve.

Missionary Handbook, p. 20.

I never liked that we were told what to write about to our own families. We were only permitted to write to them once a week on laundry day too. I vividly remember being told that we were breaking a commandment if we wrote home more than this. I never followed this rule. Whenever I wanted to vent or whenever I missed home, I would pen a letter and send it out when I was able to. Airmail was painfully slow though and our letters were always out of sync.

Today missionaries are allowed to email home on preparation day. This would have been so much better for me. However, I once had a friend serving in Canada who told me that his emails are sometimes being read by his Mission President, so he would not be able to write much anymore.

We were not allowed to watch any television or movies, read anything that was not authorised church literature, or listen to any non-Mormon music. We could not be like *E.T.* and phone home either. All we could do was read, pray, and work.

Can you imagine how miserable a mission would be if you did not get along with your companion? I felt so blessed to be learning from Elder Taylor. He was a great missionary, but he also had room for compromise. One day, we woke up at 8 a.m. instead of 6.30 a.m., and he just laughed it off. We skipped companionship study that morning and just went about our business as usual. For some reason, these mission rules did not affect me the way that the morality commandments did. I think I knew even then that God was not that petty, and that it was man-made logic being enforced on missionaries. Obedience is all about control.

One night, I was lying in bed, trying to sleep, when Elder Taylor randomly asked me if I had ever had any experience with girls. I told him that I had but that I had repented of it before I came out. There was a moment of silence and then out of nowhere, he told me he once fingered a girl in a cornfield. We both burst out laughing, and then went to sleep.

After being demoralised by the MTC, I was finally beginning to feel better about things. My companion had become a friend and we were having some success at teaching people in the area about the gospel. One man in particular, named Bruce, was really starting to respond to our visits. The only thing he was really sceptical about was the claim that we had modern day prophets and apostles leading the Church today—not to worry though; we would keep praying that his heart would soften and that the Spirit would convince him that The Church of Jesus Christ of Latter-day Saints is the only true church on the face of the earth today.

Teaching Bruce made me feel like I did when I was preparing for a mission. This was the reason I was here: not to keep nonsense hairstyle rules, and live by blind obedience alone. All I wanted to do was keep 'laying the smack down' with Elder Taylor. That is, until I had my first panic attack.

12

Panic

At 6.30 a.m., Elder Taylor's alarm woke me up, so I rolled out of bed and onto my knees and began my morning prayer. I then walked downstairs and got in the shower. I started to wash my hair when all of a sudden, my heart starting racing and I felt a wave of dread flow through me. I washed all of the shampoo out of my hair and then just stood under the water as it beat down onto my face. I felt faint and my chest felt tight. I was struggling to breathe while anxiety flooded my system. I switched the water off and just stood there shaking. I felt so afraid and I did not understand what was happening to me. After a few minutes, I began to recover, but the feeling of panic stayed with me for the whole day. I did not mention anything to Elder Taylor, although I am sure he could tell that I was slightly distracted and not quite myself.

That night, I went to sleep and started to dream that I was back home in England. I woke up in the middle of the night sweating and for a second when I opened my eyes, I thought I was in my old bedroom. When I realised where I actually was, the anxiety I had felt that morning began to drown me again. I closed my eyes and started begging God to release me from this darkness. I was convinced that this was the Devil's doing. Was this what Joseph Smith meant in his First Vision account when he said, 'I was seized upon by some power which entirely overcame me, and had such an astonishing influence over me as to bind my tongue so that I could not speak. Thick darkness gathered around me, and it seemed to me for a time as if I were doomed to sudden destruction'?

'My dear Father in Heaven, please release me from this darkness. I know Satan is trying to stop me from doing your work. Please help me feel comforted. Please help me feel okay again'. No comfort came, but I continued to pray until I fell asleep once again.

After every attack, I felt drained and I was not functioning properly. My thoughts became highly irrational and I could not shake feeling anxiety-ridden. A panic attack would be scary, but it was fleeting. It was this constant feeling of dread that I could not cope with.

One Sunday, I was struggling to get through church. I was not taking anything in and all I could think about was running away. As much as I tried to refocus myself,

I just could not concentrate on anything people were saying. I started to feel sick. I held on for as long as I was able but during a priesthood lesson, I got up and walked out of the chapel to get some fresh air. I remember trying to take deep breaths to slow down my heart rate. I was trembling and tears began to well up in my eyes. I could not do this anymore. I did not want to be here. Elder Taylor followed me out and put his arm around me and asked me how I was doing. I explained what had been happening and he advised me to speak to our Mission President.

I met with President Mathers and explained what was happening to me. He listened carefully and told me that it sounded like panic attacks. I vaguely remembered hearing that term somewhere before. When he asked me if anyone in my family also suffered with them, I knew where I had heard of the term before. 'Yes', I said. 'My dad used to get them'. I remembered that Dad had battled with panic attacks a lot before the missionaries knocked on his door. For him, Mormonism had kept them at bay. It was funny really: the Church had taken away my dad's anxiety and, all these years later, given it back to me.

I cannot remember much else about my first meeting with President Mathers, or even what he suggested I should do. He was a decent man, but he could not help himself. As I was about to leave, I heard him say, 'Oh, and Elder Yeoman, have a shave'. I had about two days of stubble on my nineteen-year-old face because I was a little preoccupied with what was happening to me. That parting comment may well have been the straw that broke the missionary's back.

As I try and sift through my mission haze, I find myself on the phone with my dad, explaining what was going on. I told him that I did not think I would be able to do this anymore and that I wanted to come home. Dad had been prepped for this conversation by church leaders and he did his best to motivate me, so I said I would try and stick it out.

President Mathers had been a little generous to me in the fact that he allowed me to call home. He also permitted me a couple of hours off from missionary work and told Elder Taylor to take me to a local diner for a milkshake. I thought, 'This must be some milkshake! I wonder if they prescribe it on the NHS?' I remember sitting in this retro diner having a strawberry milkshake and having a heart-to-heart with Taylor. I explained how I was struggling but resolved that I would carry on and try to get through it. He was really supportive and I was sorry to be a burden to him.

Back home, my family had been instructed by my Mission President and the Stake President not to write me any letters and to hang up on me if I telephoned. There is still a hole in my dad's kitchen wall from where he punched it after he was told that.

After our milkshakes, Elder Taylor and I visited a local family in the evening. They lived close by us and had done a good job feeding us and making sure I was settling in to the area. One of the family's sons was outside looking through a huge telescope at Mars, and he let us look too. He was preparing for a mission and something inside me clicked and I realised that I needed to be a better example of a missionary for him. With my new-found resolve, Elder Taylor and I were looking up at the moon and the stars and talking about the gospel and all its wonders. I started to get fired up again and realised that in the grand scheme of things, my little panic attacks were irrelevant. I told Elder Taylor that I was definitely going to stay in Roseville and continue my mission.

That night, I called home again and told Dad not to worry, everything was better. Then a day or two later, I had another panic attack, but this one left me crippled with anxiety. I felt so angry with myself, but I was even angrier at God. Why was He not responding to my prayers? I had been crying out for comfort and help and I felt nothing. It was as if God had changed His number. I did not know how to reach the great I AM anymore.

'I'm trying to serve you here!' I thought. 'I prepared in every way I could to be a missionary and now you've abandoned me! How hard is it for you to just wave your hand and take away my anxiety? Why aren't you helping me? Where are you?'

I was inwardly screaming my lungs out at Him. I had not felt the Spirit since I left England. I had come to the Mormon capital and felt nothing. I had gone to Provo and felt like I served three weeks in a robot factory. I came out to Roseville, where He had called me to serve, and now I was cursed with an anxiety disorder. This should not be mistaken for my faith wavering; it was as solid as it ever was. However, I knew for a fact that God just did not care about me anymore.

My thoughts became irrational. All I wanted to do was escape. I was sick of the constant attacks, and I was exhausted mentally and physically. I had to get back home—to hell with shaving and drinking milkshakes. I needed real help. I told Elder Taylor that I was done with it all. I could not carry on like this. I was no good to him as a companion and I was no good to the people I was trying to teach. Try as I might to fight, the time had come for flight.

Elder Taylor reported back to President Mathers and soon after, I began receiving phone calls from home. My awesome Stake President from England was calling to boost me up and to see if there was anything he could do to help me. Actually, he told me that if I came home then I would be 'letting my family down, letting my ward down, and letting the Stake down'. I got off the phone from him and my heart sank. I had respected this man so much before I left. I viewed him as a great, insightful leader, and all he had to say to me was, 'Don't come back a failure'.

My dad and my bishop also called me around this head-spinning time and told me that Dad was going to fly out to Utah. The plan was for me to get some treatment while we stayed at Mark's house and then I would be able to return to Roseville.

I spent a couple more days with Elder Taylor while arrangements were made for me to head back to Orem. I still had to engage in missionary service, so I tried to do my part the best I could. I felt so bad for letting Taylor down. I was making his mission experience hard and he deserved better than this. Before I left, we visited Bruce one last time together. I explained to Bruce that I was leaving California and going back to Utah to receive help for my panic attacks. Other than Taylor, Bruce was more concerned for my wellbeing than any Mormon out there. He did his best to make me feel like I was not failing and that my health should come first. After we got through with our lesson, I bore my testimony to him about the gospel, about Joseph Smith, and about the Book of Mormon. I bore my testimony to him that I knew that prophets and apostles were on the Earth today because God still loved and communicated with his people. I did not know why he was not communicating with me, but my anger had subsided and I felt humbled again. This was not God's fault, it was probably mine. I was hurt that my prayers were not being answered and I did not understand any of this. I viewed my last testimony to Bruce as my last chance to make a difference to someone as a missionary. Inwardly, I knew that this was the end of the road for me.

When we left Bruce's house, Elder Taylor was ecstatic and could barely contain his excitement. He could not believe how I had 'laid the smack down' like that. I felt pleased that I had helped him to have a positive experience after what I had put him through. I wondered whether maybe his next companion could pick up where I left off.

On my last day, the local bishop and the ward mission leader sat me down for one last attempt at getting me to stay in Granite Bay. They opened with prayer and started speaking. I have no recollection of anything that was said or for how long we spoke. All I can remember is one of them asking me, 'Elder Yeoman, what happens to you if your plane goes down on the way home?' What a sinister question from a grown adult to an ill nineteen-year-old boy. I remember saying that I should be fine because I could not help this and God would know that. So, I did not think I would end up in Hell for leaving my mission. How I wish for a certain time-travelling blue box, so that I could revisit that exact moment and tell them both to go fuck themselves.

I barely remember meeting with President Mathers for the last time, other than him telling me to go and get better and that he would see me soon. I thought, 'No chance mate', but I had to play along.

Elder Taylor and I spent my last day playing basketball. He challenged me to a one-on-one and was boasting that basketball is an American's game. I was so desperate to beat him but he nailed a couple of three-pointers at the death and finished me off. I told him he had an advantage because I am ill. For some reason, my last moment with Elder Taylor was also with a group of other missionaries from our area. I remember sitting in a diner with them all and feeling so small. Everyone kept asking why I was leaving.

I felt so relieved to be sitting on a small aircraft destined for San Francisco. After so much effort, I had finally been able to get away from Granite Bay. When we lifted off, I tried to get some rest. When I arrived at the airport, I bumped into some more missionaries that were also headed out to Utah, so again I had to tell them that I was leaving my mission.

I was white as a ghost when I landed in Salt Lake. I could not get my thoughts straight. Was I a failure? Could I have stuck it out? Was God mad at me? Were my family disappointed with me? I felt so many emotions, but the overriding one was the need to escape, so that was all that mattered.

Once I collected my luggage, I walked into the arrivals lobby to be greeted by a parade of Mormon families, all holding up signs and welcoming their missionaries home. For a split second, I got confused and thought they were for me, but I soon realised they were for the returning missionaries who had completed two-year missions behind me. To the left of this happy, proud group stood my dad, Mark, and Kira, all looking gloomy. As I walked over towards them and passed the other families, I wished the ground would just open, swallow me up, and plunge me straight down into a black hole where I could cease to exist.

My missionary badge, passport, Book of Mormon, and Temple Recommend.

13

Broken

Anxiety; panic attacks; the fight or flight response—these terms are so common in 2017. You would be hard-pressed to find someone that has not experienced them. Yet back when I was a missionary, recovering in Utah, I had no understanding about any of it. I knew Dad used to get panic attacks but that was it. I did not know anyone else that had them or what they were even like for other people. All I knew when I was in the States was that I felt constant dread, fear, worry, stress, and a constant desire to run away and get back home. This need to escape may seem so over the top to you, but my thinking was so irrational. I felt isolated and trapped, and home seemed so far away.

I was so glad to have Dad with me, but I knew the Church had only allowed it so that it would help my 'homesickness'. I do not think any of the leaders were concerned about my anxiety attacks; they figured that a bit of time with a family member should do the trick. Leaders had been trying to influence Dad to convince me to return to the mission field. I knew this was all going on, so in order for me to get a bit of breathing space I went along with the idea that I would be going back to Roseville after this little time-out in Utah. I could not go anywhere even if I wanted to because the Church still had my passport.

While I was in Orem, Utah, it was arranged for me to meet with a Mormon psychologist who pretty much just gave me a prescription for a drug that I cannot remember the name of and told me that if I had a panic attack, I should breathe into a brown paper bag. I was also having terrible problems sleeping, so she told me to just take deep breaths and as I exhaled to say 'sleep' in my mind. Would you be surprised to learn that none of this helped me in the slightest?

After a couple of weeks at Mark's home, I started to relax a little. I was receiving phone calls from my bishop in England and family members who were all genuinely concerned about me and not my ability to perform as a missionary. Dad was also stressed out because he kept getting heat from leaders who wanted to see me return to Roseville.

One afternoon, Dad asked me, 'If angel Moroni appeared to you right now and commanded you to go back on a mission, what would you say?' I said that

I would say no. I knew that I just could not do it anymore. My mind was too fried up and anxiety had become my new enemy, not the Devil. I was also still confused as to why God would allow this to happen to one of His servants. No one had any answers for me. After this conversation, Dad supported my decision and knew that we just needed to leave.

Church leaders were not happy about me just taking some time-out in Utah. In their eyes, I was still a missionary, and even though I was not in Roseville, I still ought to be serving. One leader called Dad up and told him that I would be going to work in a nearby Mormon canning factory. Dad rejected the idea. 'Do you know who you're talking to?' the voice on the phone retorted.

'I'm a relative of the prophet Wilford Woodruff!'

'I don't care if you're the pope! He's not doing it.' Dad replied and hung up the phone.

The Holy Ghost was like a long-lost friend to me. Anxiety was now my constant companion. I felt highly strung, always on the verge of a breakdown, and depression began to set in. I no longer cared who I might be letting down. I was ill and leaders seemed more concerned about whether I had shaved or if I was still reading my scriptures and praying daily.

To make matters more unsettling, we soon discovered that there was tension in the home we were staying in. Mark and his wife were on the verge of separating and sometimes we would get caught in the family's crossfire. On one occasion, Mark lashed out at his wife and Dad intervened. The missionary that had converted my parents was then rolling around on the floor, fighting with Dad. I threw Mark off and screamed at him in un-missionary-like language. He stormed out of his house and I think ended up staying in a hotel. I threw my missionary badge against the wall and said I was finished with it. Kira was also having issues with her dad, and it was just an awkward position for us to be in. We were trying to make sense of what was happening to me, and now we had to try and navigate our way through family drama that we had no business being involved in. Dad was stressed out too and started to get ill. I remember us both just sitting in silence in our shared bedroom, wishing this nightmare would end.

One morning, I got so sick of people trying to tell me that I should be going back to Roseville that I stormed out of Mark's house and went for a walk to get away from all the crap that was going on. Kira followed me out and took my hand and eventually walked me back. Some nosey Mormon in the area with nothing better to do with their life reported me to the Church and I was chastised for holding her hand as a missionary.

After this, I started to announce that in my mind, I was no longer a missionary and I would not be held accountable for any of those ridiculous mission rules anymore. Meanwhile, Dad kept inquiring about the whereabouts of my passport. We were not going anywhere until the Church gave it back to me, and they knew that.

The medication I was taking was not helping and neither were the counselling sessions. The Church was at a loss for how to help me. As one final attempt, they asked my Dad if there was anyone else who may be able to help change my mind about going home. Dad mentioned a General Authority's name, and said that I loved him. I had his books and talk-tapes back home and if anyone could make a difference then it might be him. He was not an apostle, but he was a member of the Quorum of the Seventy at this time. Even though Dad knew that it would not change my mind, he thought it would at least be a nice experience while I was out there to meet one of my Mormon heroes and maybe get some spiritual council from him.

Soon after this, we went to Church Headquarters in Salt Lake City so that I could meet one-on-one with this General Authority whom I had admired, in his office. I wish I could report that this was a positive experience for me, but it was the total opposite. He could not understand why I was having panic attacks and feeling so anxious that I would want to leave the mission field and return home. He did not even consider the possibility that it may be a legitimate illness. Instead, he deemed it to be a spiritual problem. He asked me if I had any unresolved guilt. Was there something that occurred before my mission that I needed to repent of? I told him that I had repented of my sins long before I came on a mission and that I had not done anything that needed to be reconciled since.

He then asked me what those past sins where. I found this to be an inappropriate question for him to ask because when you repent and you are forgiven, in God's eyes, it is like the sin never even happened, so why did I need to retell them? I went ahead and told him about my past sins with immorality and felt so ashamed and embarrassed. I could not believe I had to tell this spiritual giant all my dirty little secrets. Now he would think I was a terrible Mormon and he would not look at me in the way I had hoped. After I went through my past transgressions and assured him that I had confessed them to my bishop, he asked me about holding hands with Kira. I was shocked that he even knew about that. How had it been reported all the way to Church HQ? I explained that it was just an innocent, kind gesture from Kira to help calm me down.

Seemingly at a loss, he then asked me if I was gay. I was so confused by this question, but I told him that I was not. What was going on here? He must be so desperate to find a reason to blame me for what was happening. Everything else is a blur. I know he gave me a priesthood blessing before I left his office and my dad assisted. The blessing was basic and generic and left us feeling icy cold. For a General Authority, he had no spiritual discernment. He had no idea how to help me or how to bless me. In his books and in his talks, you would think he was like one of the twelve disciples, but in person, face-to-face, he had the inspiration of a blunt shovel. Dad chucked this man's books and tapes out in the bin when he got home, and we have never been impressed with the status of 'General Authority' ever since. That was the final slap in the face for Dad. He demanded my passport be returned to me immediately or he would go to the press.

I think I was given my passport back when I met with President Freeman, a councillor serving in Orem's Stake Presidency. He was the only leader who showed me any compassion and support out there. When he was younger, he had decided to get married instead of serving a mission, so he was very empathetic to how I was feeling. He told me to go home and get better. Arrangements were then made for me and Dad to fly home.

I cannot even remember how long we ended up staying at Mark's, but it seemed like an eternity. While I was out there and before the fight, Mark kindly took Dad and me on a trip to see some sights. We drove through Arizona, saw the Hoover Dam and the Grand Canyon, and spent a couple of nights in Caesar's Palace in Las Vegas. I know that I have been to all of these places, but my memory of them is foggy. I was going through so much emotional turmoil that I cannot say I enjoyed any of it.

After the fight at Mark's, he did not stay at the house, so we did not even say goodbye to him. His wife and Kira took us to Salt Lake City airport when the time came for us to leave. I hugged Kira goodbye and boarded the plane. She was a sweet girl and I was glad to have her friendship during one of the most difficult times of my life. When the plane sat on the runway waiting to take off, I sobbed like a child. I could not wait to get home.

14

Home

A family friend picked us up from the airport. The ride home was sombre, as if we had been collected from a funeral. After watching the green of England flash by the car windows for a while, I fell asleep. When I woke up, we were home. I hugged my mum and brother tight when I saw them. They had also gone through a stressful time worrying about me and Dad. I was finally where I had longed to be for so long.

It took me a little while to adjust to civilian life. My brother was showing me bands that I had never heard of and catching me up on movies I had missed out on. It felt good to be home and back with my family, but I was not the same person as the one that left. I began to withdraw and I felt distracted. I could not concentrate on much and I was still feeling stressed out by the Church.

My Mission President and my local leaders were still under the impression that I would return to Roseville after I had recovered from my anxiety struggles. I remember receiving an email from President Mathers, telling me to get better and to come back when I was able to. I also remember him telling me not to go inactive from the Church because of what had happened.

Over the next few weeks, I received several visits from my local leaders and various members of the Church who had heard that I had come home. My bishop was genuinely concerned about me, but his spiritual guidance no longer had any effect on me. I did not want to hear any theories about why God had allowed this to happen. I was sick of being told that I was not a failure too. Two people whom I used to count as friends paid me a visit, but they could not have been any more obvious about why they came to see me. They didn't care about me; they just wanted to know why I was home.

Members from my own ward began to gossip and rumours began to circulate about why I had come home. Some people were saying that my family was too close and that I was just homesick. Others were saying that I had shared sexual relations with Kira, and so I had been sent home due to transgression. Despite this slander, I still found the ability to attend church on Sundays. I am sure some members did show me some support and love, but I only remember the bad things now. I was viewed as a failure and an embarrassment to my Stake President. People just assumed that a panic attack was being short of breath and needing to breathe into a paper bag. They had no idea about the emotional turmoil I had suffered and was still suffering with. It seemed to me that every talk and lesson was about missionary work. I ended up walking out and getting Dad to take me home a lot of the time. Eventually, I decided that I needed a break from church as everything just felt too raw.

When leaders finally got the message that I was not going to return to Roseville, there was talk about me serving the remainder of my mission in the UK. Again, it was this insulting notion that if I was closer to home I may cope better that really started to piss me off. I was homesick, but no more or less than any other missionary. The fact was I could not control my anxiety and my mental health became a priority to me. I could not function as a missionary, and I could not see any light at the end of the tunnel, so I debunked any further talk of me serving any kind of mission. Other than close friends, I did not want to be around any Mormons for a while.

I was released from my calling as a missionary and I received an official letter from the Church, informing me that I had been released with honour. I felt like photocopying the letter and handing them out at church. 'Here, have a look!' I thought. 'I was honourably released, so how about shutting your gossiping mouths now?'

One Sunday, a friend of my dad's left church early to come and see him. He had heard people slating me for being home. Dad put on his suit and drove to church.

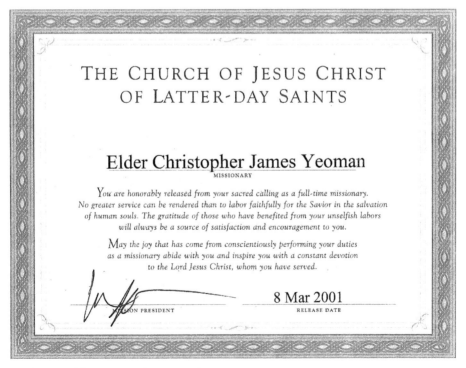

THE CHURCH OF JESUS CHRIST
OF LATTER-DAY SAINTS

Elder Christopher James Yeoman
MISSIONARY

You are honorably released from your sacred calling as a full-time missionary. No greater service can be rendered than to labor faithfully for the Savior in the salvation of human souls. The gratitude of those who have benefited from your unselfish labors will always be a source of satisfaction and encouragement to you.

May the joy that has come from conscientiously performing your duties as a missionary abide with you and inspire you with a constant devotion to the Lord Jesus Christ, whom you have served.

MISSION PRESIDENT

8 Mar 2001
RELEASE DATE

My honourable mission release certificate.

It happened to be a testimony meeting, so he got up at the pulpit and blasted the ward. He then resigned from his calling as counsellor on the bishopric.

When I had been home for about a month, I got a phone call from Elder Kent. He had heard that I had left Roseville and he wanted me to know that I had pulled him through the MTC. He told me that my coming home did not change his opinion of me in the slightest. We spoke for a long time. He said he was also finding his mission tough. I later found out that Elder Kent also left Roseville and went home early.

I also got a letter in the mail from Elder Taylor:

Dear Chris,

What's up? How you doing? I hope everything is going good for you. I have to tell you a few good things that happened after you left. Bruce was baptized! He then didn't come to church for a while, but he is going to church now. Since you left I trained another missionary and right now I'm serving as a zone leader in the Roseville Zone. I also broke a bone in my elbow playing basketball last preparation day, so I'm out for a little while.

I just wanted to tell you that you are the best! Serving with you was some of the funnest times on my whole mission. All of the girls in the ward were asking where you were after you were gone. You made quite the impression!

How is everything back in England? How is your family doing? Tell them I say hi, and tell them thank you for raising a good young man such as yourself.

You're the best companion I've had. We got along so well. Just remember basketball is America's game. I just wanted to remind you of that.

Well, I better let you go. You're the best, and I love you son.

Love,

Elder Taylor.

P. S. Get some English ladies for me.

Somehow, my MTC companion also heard that I had come home. I am not sure how exactly because he went to Chicago. His letter spoke about his wet dreams and him wanking to Britney; I did not write back to him. I wondered how it was fair that someone like him was happily serving a mission, and how someone like me could not.

Dad was fiercely protective of me as I began my recovery. One of the first things he did was tear the Stake President a new one for telling me that I was letting everyone down—how dare he speak on behalf of his family, and tell a sick young man he was a let-down in his hour of need. The Stake President apologised to me and I let it go. What I did not know then was that during that time, he was committing adultery; the man in charge of over 1,000 local Mormons was a fraud. He was cheating on his wife with his best friend's wife and pretending to be an inspired leader called by God for years. I could not believe this hypocrite had the nerve to chastise me. I was fooled by his leadership and lies. I am not quite sure how members in my area can blindly trust their leaders after that. I have heard some of them say, 'Even though he wasn't worthy, the Spirit still worked through him for the benefit of the Stake'—the things people tell themselves to avoid the cold hard truth.

I also discovered that the bishop who told me in my youth to visualise the nails being smashed into Christ's hands had also committed adultery and fled to America after he had been excommunicated. This man called me up from Utah when I came home from my mission and asked me to come out there and stay with him. He said the members there were much more forgiving and less judgemental. He had been re-baptised and he wanted to help me. Without even needing to think about it, I declined his offer. I never wanted to see Utah again.

My current bishop was still showing me support. He respected that I did not want any spiritual dialogue anymore but he was keen to get me professional help for my anxiety. He funded a couple of sessions with a non-Mormon psychologist who informed me that I had suffered a nervous breakdown. He also kept me on the drug that I had been prescribed in the States. I did not find the sessions helpful, if anything they frustrated me, and so I stopped going. I decided to just see my GP and stay on medication that was supposed to treat my anxiety and depression. I remained on this drug for about a year and I became numb, angry, and I started to withdraw from everyone around me. I was also feeling suicidal and getting frequent panic attacks. I was later told that one in four people had killed themselves after being on the drug I was taking, so I came off it cold turkey and went through an awful withdrawal period. I would get what I used to describe as head-shocks. All of a sudden, I would get a sensation like a ghost had passed right through me. My head would ache, I would get a massive wave of butterflies, and I would feel dizzy. It was a weird sensation. My thoughts were all over the place and this made me more anxious. I found it difficult to sleep so I would sometimes take Vallium to give myself some rest. It was a hard time for my family seeing me so messed up.

I got to a point where I no longer wanted to do anything other than stay in my room where I would spend the day painting, listening to music, and watching *Buffy the Vampire Slayer*. Sometimes, my friends would come and hang out with me, but I was miserable company. When my anxiety was not boiling over into a panic attack, it was always simmering away inside. I tried to seem as normal as possible around people but I just wanted to hide away in my room. I could not convey what I was going through and I found quick-fix advice intolerable.

My family was still going out to church but I could not face it. I was no longer praying or reading scripture. I was finding comfort in comic books and art instead. I was no longer feeling any guilt about what music I was listening to or what movies I was watching either. A lot of people thought that it was the medication I was on, which had made me numb to the Spirit. Maybe it was, but I was glad about it. I was too ill to worry about my soul. I did not need the burden of a Mormon conscience, and I was sick of the Church.

15

The Devil Must Have Heard

After several months of hiding away and feeling sorry for myself, I began to socialise with more of my non-Mormon friends. I ended up going out to alternative night clubs, which became a welcomed distraction from religion. My passion for music began to soothe my wounds. I began to live for the weekend. Most of my new friends were 'straight edge', which meant that they abstained from drugs, alcohol, and promiscuous sex—what an ideal crowd for an inactive Mormon who still wanted to keep the Word of Wisdom. I soon bonded with this crowd and we had a lot of fun dancing the night away and chasing girls. Despite being inactive, I still had a testimony of Mormonism. I knew it to be true; I had just come to terms with the fact that I could not be around judgemental, gossiping 'Christians' anymore. I wanted to forget my mission, and my new friends were helping me do that.

One night at a local metal club, I was dancing near a pretty blonde named Jess. A friend of hers came up to me and said that Jess liked me. Of course, I said I liked her back, and so he introduced us. I kissed Jess for a while and at the end of the night, she gave me her number. We texted the following week and met up again at another club before I eventually went over to her house. Jess was keen to start seeing me officially, but I was reluctant to get into a relationship because I knew that my Mormon ways probably would not be fun for her. She wanted to give it a try and so we ended up dating. I fell in love really fast and lost my virginity to her. For the first time in my life, I did not feel any guilt, remorse, or shame. I did not feel the need to ask God for mercy. I felt great and I made up for lost time.

I think it was a surprise to people that I was not feeling any guilt about having sex. They did not want to accept that I just did not feel bad about it; they blamed my medication for blocking out my conscience instead.

As I was feeling happier and had something positive in my life, I went through a weird phase of believing that I had God's approval. He knew what I had been through and He knew that I was in love. This was not just casual sex; it meant something. I started to pray again and tried to rebuild my fractured relationship with my Heavenly Father. It was a weird position to be in. I had a testimony, I kept all the other commandments, I just was not going out to church anymore, and I was having sex. This made me an enigma for Jess and caused problems for us as a couple. Like a regular person at her age, she liked to drink and smoke on occasion, but it offended my 'straight edge' Mormon ways, so it caused tension. Jess was sweet enough to remedy this by pretty much adopting a straight edge lifestyle so that we could be in harmony, but if she ever did have an alcoholic drink or a cigarette, I would feel betrayed. It sounds utterly moronic to me now, but I was not in the healthiest state of mind to be in a normal functioning relationship.

I felt that Jess was too wild for me and I could not quite keep up with her. Religious roots were still wrapped around my ankles and they kept tripping me over. I was too arrogant to see myself as the problem; instead, I expected her to change because of my faith.

I was still suffering from panic attacks during this time and I found it difficult to balance my love for Jess and my love for a religion that had broken me. I suppose I was having an identity crisis and I never really knew where I belonged anymore. No matter how much I tried to escape my faith, it would always come back to haunt me.

I was in Jess's bed when I found out about 9/11. Someone phoned me and told me what had happened. Jess went downstairs and turned on the news while I sat up in bed being told it was 'the last days and the Second Coming was near'. I remember feeling a mixture of emotions. I did not really take in what had happened to the Twin Towers until after when I went downstairs and saw the images on the television for myself. My first thoughts were fear of not being ready for judgement day, and then anger at it being used to scare me back to church.

I tried my best to adapt to life outside of Mormonism, but I could not get the indoctrination out of my system. Jess once asked me if she thought I would ever marry her, and I said I doubted it because I needed to marry someone in the Temple. These little wedges became too much for us in the end. I was judgemental of the people she was hanging around with, and I could not deal with her ex-boyfriends sniffing around. I began to be paranoid, possessive, and I began to lose trust in her. I was jealous of her past and I could not handle that she had not been as 'pure' as me. I had been conditioned to believe that I was to marry a worthy daughter of God, someone who had saved themselves for marriage. My insecurities made me someone that I detested. Towards the end of the relationship, we argued a lot and Jess finally ended it. I was heartbroken and tried desperately to get back together but she was through with me. She told me that I should find a Mormon girl to make me happy.

Since my mission, I had lost all sense of myself and had invested everything I had left in our relationship, so I was absolutely crushed. It took a couple of years for me to get over her. I started dating other girls, but I would break up with them early on because they were not Jess. I was a selfish asshole and I probably hurt a lot of people's feelings back then. Jess did not help me either though. Whenever I started to feel strong, she would call me up and see how I was doing. She could not quite let me go either. I became so angry that she would torture me like this and not have me back so I yelled at her to never contact me again. I called her horrible things that I have felt bad for ever since.

I felt broken all over again. One day, I felt so humbled and upset that I turned back to the Lord for help. I told Him that I was sorry for turning away from His love and that I had learned my lesson. I tried to go back to church, but it just did not feel the same to me anymore, so I would just live the gospel inwardly for now.

Soon after my breakup with Jess, I went to Greece for two weeks with my family and family friends. I carried my heartache across the Atlantic Ocean, but I did my best to enjoy my time there in the gorgeous sunshine.

My brother and one of our best friends, Marcus, had a lot of fun together writing songs and messing around in the ocean. We spent our days watching movies in bars and eating the most amazing kebabs, and at night, we would walk around hoping to meet girls.

One evening, I spent a good hour walking and talking with Marcus's dad about returning to church. He told me that when I got home, I should make an appointment with the new bishop and get the repentance process rolling. I felt vulnerable at the time, so I committed to doing exactly that, but the Devil must have heard. Later that night, I met a girl and ended up having sex with her on the beach at sunrise. We exchanged names after the act and she asked if I was up for it again that night. I lied and said I was going home that afternoon.

I crawled back into bed that morning, feeling sick with myself. I did not know why I had done it. I wanted to get Jess out of my system, but I also just thought, 'To hell with it'. I lay in bed for a while, feeling dirty and ashamed with myself. I offered up some half-hearted repentance prayer to God and then vowed that when I did get back to England I would confess my sins to the new bishop.

Jess contacted me a few more times after I got home and then disappeared. I soon transformed my anger at her by turning her into a regret. I would repent of my sins and finally exorcise the demon.

The new bishop was nothing like the last one. This bishop was, in my opinion, unqualified to have jurisdiction over so many Latter-day saints. He was power hungry and uninspired, his council was dangerous at times, and he did not have an ounce of mercy.

Many people complained about this bishop over the years that he was in office, but the Stake Presidency would rebuke anyone who 'spoke out against the Lord's anointed'—I hate that phrase with every fibre of my being. The Church forbids its leaders to be questioned or criticised. In 2007, a Latter-day Saint apostle even said: 'It's wrong to criticise leaders of the Church, even if that criticism is true'—well is that not just great?

To speak out against the Lord's anointed is considered to be a sin. Even when people agreed with me that something was wrong, they would say to me, 'Well try and respect the office if you can't respect the man. The Lord's called him to be bishop, so that's that'. Called by God? Through whom? Of course, the Stake President, who was having an affair.

I was feeling in the depths of guilt and sorrow again when I met with the bishop for the first time. He was aware of my mission experience; my anxiety and depression; and that when I had sinned, it had been during my inactive period from church. He asked me how many times I had slept with Jess. I thought that was an odd question, so I just said there was nine months' worth of sex. As much as I had wanted to make Jess a regret, I knew I was lying to myself. I did not regret sleeping with her, I just knew that I was supposed to be feeling guilty about it. I was feeling humble because I was heartbroken and sorrowful because I had rebelled against God and got burned for it. I did feel grimy about the one-off in Greece though, so I also got that off of my chest and showed the bishop genuine guilt.

The actual interview was okay. He was easy enough to talk to and he did not make me feel bad; it was just that he did not show me any compassion or understanding. The price I had to pay for breaking my temple covenants was too severe. The bishop put me on something called 'probation', which meant that I was not allowed a church calling, I was not allowed to partake of the sacrament, and I was not allowed to assist in any priesthood ordinances. I would also have to meet with the bishop every so often for review.

Being put on probation undid any progress I had made about feeling any self-worth. I felt unworthy again, just like before my mission. 'O wretched man that I am'. I wanted to draw close to God again, but I knew that it was going to be a long road ahead. The bishop made me feel that I had to prove my commitment to God again before I could obtain forgiveness, and I could not understand it.

During Christ's ministry on earth, He would forgive people on the spot. On one occasion, Jesus came across an adulterous woman and simply said, 'Go and sin no more'. Even on the cross, Jesus forgave those who had crucified Him. He then turned to a crucified thief and told him that he would soon be with Him in Paradise. All throughout the scriptures, there are examples of how God would instantly forgive those who turned unto Him. No one felt as sorry as I did about my sinful state, so why did I have to endure the humiliation of probation?

The bishop watched me like a hawk and even seemed to enjoy having this power over me. If I missed church, a fireside, or a lesson, he would call me up on it and delay my release from probation.

On one occasion, I skipped part of a Sunday school lesson to talk to a few friends outside of the building. My friend Marcus and his sister Jane (who I also grew up with because our families were so close) were outside with us. We had only been out there talking for a few minutes, when suddenly out of nowhere the bishop came storming over to us and started shooing us back in the building. He was mad at me in particular and told me that it was inappropriate for me to be with Jane considering I was on probation. I was horrified by this ugly accusation. Jane was much younger than me and had been a family friend for over a decade, and here was my bishop shouting at me like I was some sick sexual predator. I was insulted and disgusted by his warped mind.

My dad was furious at the bishop and detested him as a person. They would often be on the phone arguing with each other about his conduct and the length of my probation. It was being dragged out for far too long.

I began to lose heart and so my church attendance dropped. I did not like the bishop and I do not believe he liked me or my family much either.

16

The Samurai Summer

During my probationary period, I started socialising a lot with my brother's friends. It was the summer holidays and they were practically living at my parents' house. I must have been about twenty and they were all about sixteen or seventeen. They were all Mormons and a good bunch of lads. We got up to all sorts of things that summer, mainly visiting haunted locations and writing songs together. For some reason, one of the lads started calling us the 'Samurais', and that was what we became known as to our peers at church. Our reputation as a 'gang' got so far-fetched and ridiculous that our group was raised as a point of concern in a church leadership meeting. This did not help my case with the bishop either. He told me that he found it weird that I was hanging about with younger people and I that should get friends my own age. He really was a dickhead.

My friends who were 'my own age' just were not around. I lost contact with most of my straight edge friends because I did not go to the clubs anymore. Tim was serving a mission in the UK, and my other best mate, Josh, was away at university.

I recently found a letter that Tim sent me while he was on his mission. We must have made a pact not to masturbate because he asked: 'How is it man? How are you doing on our pact? Let me know dude. I've found it hard.' Well, that is not a good start, Tim. 'But seriously have gained strength in the time of need from knowing that we promised each other. Mate, it's seriously hard isn't it?!' I certainly agreed with that. 'This thing ain't gonna let up easily, but we have to beat it.' That was what we were trying not to do, buddy.

Mate I'll totally understand if you've not quite managed it. If you haven't start again now—there ain't no better time than now. Each moment we can start afresh because of Christ. Let me know either way so I can gain some strength. It's all about the mind isn't it? We can beat this bro!

I was trying not to, I really was. 'Anyway dude, hit me back with a letter.'

Josh had also suffered some Mormon shaming while I was at college. He had decided to go to university instead of a mission. I remember at the time even I felt a little judgemental about his decision; he had begun filling in his mission papers and then, all of a sudden, changed his mind. Josh is a little older than me and he has always been one step ahead of me in our journey to the dark side of the Force.

Josh lost his virginity at university; after, he sat on the end of the bed and wept. We joke about this today, but in all seriousness, I am livid that Mormonism caused us all such grief. I wish that religious guilt had not ruined our teenage years. Today, Josh is happily married to his beautiful wife and they have two wonderful boys. The best thing he ever did was skip his mission call, but he still paid for professional counselling to undo his Mormon indoctrination.

Tim also sought out professional help. I did not know until years later, but he had suffered with schizophrenia on his mission. It went undiagnosed and untreated because he kept it to himself. He wanted to be an honourable missionary and so he somehow managed to stick at it for the whole two years. Years later, he had a nervous breakdown and suffered a terrible ordeal with his illness. He is still recovering today. While Tim was on his mission, someone close to him asked Josh and I not to write to him in case our negative influence affected him—how charming.

So, with Tim and Josh away from home, I was glad to be one of the 'Samurais'. We were obsessed with trekking out late at night to an old abandoned house nearby to where my parents lived. It was a white, sinister-looking house that had three floors with no doors or windows, just open frames, which were pitch-black and looked menacing from the outside. It was out of the way in a woodland area and at night it looked terrifying. We used to scare the hell out of each other there while trying to find ghosts. When we realised that it was not actually haunted, we started to make our own fun by bringing new people there. We spray-painted the walls with pentagrams and dark lyrics to add to the effect. When we would bring new people to the house, one of us would already be waiting in the basement to make noises and haunt the new visitors. Some people would not even dare go into the house when they saw it, and those that did usually ran out screaming. Someone in our group decided it would be a good idea to take a dump in the middle of one of the rooms to create the scent of death. We instantly knew it was a mistake and so he was then tasked with removing it from the premises.

We spent so many nights running around that house. On one occasion, my brother fell through a hole in the third floor and down to the second floor. He broke his nose but was lucky that he did not come off any worse. I felt so guilty on the walk home that night because he had not wanted to come out in the first place but I had made him. As the moon climbed high into the cool night sky, he clicked his nose back into place and grumbled at me. I apologised for making him come out and put my arm around him. 'You've got blood on my favourite hat though', I said, as we walked across a field under a starlit sky towards home.

When we were not at the not-so-haunted-house, we would walk around the woods and the local golf course. It was a suspicious sight to see seven or eight of us walking around at 2 a.m. We would often get stopped by police and questioned. One time, we had been discussing the Church and a police car pulled up and asked us what we were doing. One of the boys said we were talking about Jesus Christ, and I am pretty sure the officers thought we had been smoking weed.

On another occasion, we were sitting on a bench somewhere at 1 a.m. when we decided it would be fun to drop our trousers when the next car came by. The headlights appeared and we did it. Blue lights started flashing and we realised that we had just flashed the police. The car pulled a huge U-turn and headed for us as we ran away trying to get our jeans back up. We split up and ran for cover. We hid in the woods for a while and then slowly made our way back to my house through the back roads. I know it was juvenile behaviour, but I had not done anything silly for years—except go back to church.

These were the days when we were all using MSN messenger. One evening while I was online, a brunette with gorgeous brown eyes started talking to me through a mutual friend's account. She said her name was Kym and my profile had caught her attention. We chatted for a while and she told me that she was on the verge of breaking up with her boyfriend. After that conversation, we became friends and eventually arranged to meet up one afternoon. By the time we did meet, Kym had broken up with her boyfriend and we hit it off right away. I was still a little guarded at the time and was not looking for a relationship, but I was glad that Kym was in my life.

Around this time, Jess phoned me and asked if we could meet up to try and achieve some closure. She came to town one afternoon and we sat on a wall somewhere and had an awkward conversation. Jess showed me a photo of her new boyfriend and I did my best to pretend I was happy for her. As I walked her back to the train station, Kym called and asked if I wanted to meet up with her. I hugged Jess goodbye for the last time and then went to see Kym.

A couple of months later, I went to a house party to hang out with Kym and we ended up spending the whole night talking in her friend's bedroom. We finally admitted that we both liked each other, but I was really cautious about getting into a relationship. I did not want to let her down or hurt her like I had the other girls I had tried dating after Jess. I was bad with commitment and I was still on church probation. I could not afford to slip up again and so I explained to her all about my religion and what it required of me. Kym was sympathetic to my fears and said it was refreshing to meet someone like me. We decided to take things slow and see how things went. We fell asleep at about 5 a.m. and then Kym got up a couple of hours later for work. The next night, I saw her again and we kissed for the first time. At the time of writing this, we have been together for fifteen years and happily married for twelve of them. However, we had a bumpy beginning.

17

Sin, Repent, Repeat

The bishop should have taken me off probation months before I even met Kym. I believe that if I had been allowed to function as a normal member of the Church, I may have had more motivation and strength, but I hated my ward. In hindsight, I wish I had just squashed my testimony into the dirt and got on with my life as a normal human being. My mission experience should have been enough for me to never go back, but the indoctrination was deeply rooted and I still could not escape its clutches.

Kym and I fell in love early on into our relationship. I was still emotionally all over the place, but she was compassionate and patient with my flaws. We did not have sex until our wedding night, but we did everything else leading up to it. Early on, I did not bother repenting for what we got up to because I thought of myself as inactive again and I blocked out what God may be thinking or what the bishop would say if he found out.

This changed though when Kym became interested in joining the Church. She asked my parents if she could attend church with them one Sunday and asked me to teach her about it all. I began by telling her about Joseph Smith and the Book of Mormon, and pretty much taught her the first discussion in my bedroom. She became really receptive to it all and wanted the missionaries to teach her. At this time, Kym had been through a lot in her life and was suffering with depression. The gospel began to help her cope with her experiences and she received a priesthood blessing, which seemingly dispelled her depression. Who was I to stand in her way? If she was to join the Church, then I could marry her. I decided that I ought to pull my act together and so I really began to try to reignite my faith. I started praying again and reading from the scriptures. I began to attend church with my family and Kym, and those old familiar feelings began to return to me. Like a fool, I made the mistake of confessing to the bishop that I had sinned again and that I needed to repent. I should not have done it, but I soon became tormented once again, like I was before my mission about my sins. I knew that confession led to forgiveness, so I trusted that the Lord would bless me for doing the right thing. Instead, my probation was extended and my apparent desire to change and start afresh did not mean anything to the bishop.

We had two really good missionaries in our ward at the time; they soon bonded with Kym and taught her the discussions. As Kym's testimony in the restored gospel grew, she desired to be baptised into the Church. When I reflect on this, I am glad she did because there is a good chance that we may not have made it as a couple had she not. Despite my contradictory relationship with the Church, I would probably have always wanted a Mormon wife.

Kym asked me to baptise her, but because I was on probation, I was not allowed to. I spent so much personal time repenting for my sins and recommitting myself to live the commandments. I immersed myself in spirituality all over again. Kym and I would pray and study together. My family restarted Family Home Evenings, and we all became really close and happy that things were finally feeling a little more like they did before my mission call.

Kym had saved me from the despair I had felt. Her love and friendship really made me feel like a person who had worth again. I felt like Kym had converted me back to church, just as much as I had converted her. We felt blessed to have found one another and both of our lives were better for it. My relationship with God was stronger than it ever was. I really felt like he had blessed me with Kym. Had I been on a mission, we would never have met, so maybe there was some divine purpose in me coming home early.

Bruce had been baptised. He even phoned me to thank me for sharing my testimony with him before I left. I started to wonder if that was all that I had needed to do before baptising my future wife. I did not feel like a failure anymore. I felt like I had done some good in the end. Now that I had softened my heart, the Spirit was able to reach me. I felt so warm again, like I had just walked out from darkness into the light. When I prayed, I felt like God was listening again, and when I read the scriptures, they spoke to my soul like they used to. I was absolutely buzzing that I had found a way back to the Lord. When I prayed, I felt forgiven of my sins, so I stopped repenting. Instead, I started asking God how I could serve Him better. I was so relieved to be out of the depths of despair that I arranged to meet the bishop to tell him that I was free.

The bishop sat in my parent's living room and listened to me talk about how I was feeling. I told him that I knew that God had forgiven me, so it was time to be released from probation and time for Kym to get baptised. 'The thing is, Chris, I don't know that you're forgiven. God will tell me when you are,' he said. I could not believe what I was hearing. How dare he come between me and God? I knew in my heart that I was redeemed and I knew that God wanted Kym to be baptised into His church. I told him again that it did not matter if he did not know because I knew. He told me that I was still on probation and I was so mad. I could not believe that he was pissing all over my personal revelation like this. After being high as a kite, I felt punctured and deflated.

My dad was sick of this unfair treatment. He spoke with the bishop himself and explained how the medication I had been prescribed had affected my character and judgement, and that this ought to be taken into consideration when reviewing my case. The bishop thanked my dad for letting him know about that and said that it did make a difference. He would pray about it and was sure I would be off probation soon enough.

The next night, the bishop phoned Dad and said, 'Ah, you almost got me, Bob. You almost tricked me. How dare you bully me like that. I've prayed about it and I now realise that it was the spirit of Satan that you were using last night, but Chris won't be coming of it yet.' Dad blew his gasket and decided enough was enough; you could not reason with someone like that. He went over the bishop's head and phoned the Stake President and explained everything that was going on. Soon after, the Stake President met with me before church and I explained what had been happening and how I felt. He was kind and sympathetic. I think he felt guilty about how he had handled my mission and he reached out to me with empathy and love. He said that I had been on probation 'For far too long, and it was time for it to end'. I felt so relieved and I thanked him for being understanding. I knew God had forgiven me, so who was anyone to stand in the way of that?

Later that day, the bishop asked to speak with me and said 'I've prayed about it, and the Lord has told me that it's time for you to come off probation'. I knew this was utter bullcrap. He had not received inspiration; the Stake President had forced his hand. I was so glad to be free from his clutches.

The next degrading part about this whole process was that I could not just be taken off it so easily; I had to attend a Church Disciplinary Court (CDC), where my case would be reviewed to see if I was worthy enough to be set free. I had to attend because it would look like I was not sincere if I did not. I remember standing in a chapel, looking at Tim's mission photos and letters to his ward on a noticeboard and asking the Lord for some strength. I felt sick, like a spiritual criminal awaiting my pending fate.

Whenever I cannot remember a church memory, I know it is because it was traumatic for me and so it gets lost in the haze for my own protection. I cannot remember much about the CDC, except for how I felt: degraded, humiliated, and like dirt.

Just as the Court was closing, the bishop asked if anyone else wanted to ask me anything. His first councillor said, 'Yes, actually, Chris, could you bear your testimony to us?' My stomach sank and I felt rage coursing through my veins. Did these people get off on making people feel beneath them? You power hungry bastards. I took a moment to compose myself and started to blurt out everything they wanted to hear. It was not an honest or sincere testimony, I was just saying the usual bullshit Mormon testimony phrases so that I could finally escape this spiritual prison sentence. 'Thank you', he said. Fuck you.

I was finally free. I told myself never to confess to this man ever again. 'I don't care if you find yourself in a ten-woman orgy, you never give this bishopric a bean ever again Yeoman!' I thought.

On Sunday, 23 March 2003, I baptised Kym into The Church of Jesus Christ of Latter-day Saints. It was a special moment for us and the start of our new adventure together. After Kym was baptised, the bishop offered a few words, but again, out of nowhere, he asked me if I would get up and bear my testimony. I had not spoken in church since my mission, but I threw my suit jacket off and got up at the pulpit anyway. I cannot remember what I said, but it was Kym's day, not his.

Kym fully invested herself into Mormon life and we grew closer together as the months rolled by, but we were both in love and human, and so things began to happen. As my state of mind was very much like it was pre-mission, I began to be destroyed by guilt again. It was worse this time though because I now felt responsible for two people. I felt like I was letting Kym down every time things went a little too far. 'I should be a better example to her.' I thought. 'I should be stronger now.'

I knew that I would never confess anything to the bishop again so I always felt like my repentance was only 75 per cent complete, which caused me more emotional anguish. The way I got through it was by promising myself that I would confess to the next bishop in line, and that way, I would eventually have completed all of the repentance steps. Maybe then, I would make it to heaven in the next life. For now, all I could do was confess to God and keep trying to change my behaviour. Is it not curious that when I was inactive, I felt no guilt or remorse for my sins, but anytime I was a fully active Mormon, I was burdened by guilt?

I am going to include some journal entries now so that you can see how scrambled my mind was during this time. When I first read them back, I was shocked at how unhealthy my thought process was.

I am not clean or acceptable in God's view. If I died right now I am in Hell for eternity. This scares me so much. I don't understand why I would be sent to misery because I slipped this month in a few ways? I know that no unclean thing can dwell with God. I know 'I wouldn't feel comfortable in His presence'. I know all these sayings and facts, but am I not a son of God, who is struggling so much to stop feeling sick? My heart wants to do good, but that won't matter. I sin because I'm human; I choose the 'easy' way sometimes, but I want to stay close to the Lord. I have cried and pleaded that I won't hurt anymore. I've prayed so many times, but ten months later I'm still tortured. Due to this I become weak, I sin, I'm unworthy, I repent, I try and try again, I get tired of working to get the Spirit, so I collapse. Now why should I go to Hell for this? I don't want to go there. I need to talk to the Lord, I need him to talk to me, to reach in my heart and take out this pain, to change me, to touch me so I'm pure and clean to embrace me so I'm comforted, to give me strength, to let me be a rock, instead of insecure, to touch my eyes so I won't look back. To change my

Dressed in white for Kym's baptism, 2003.

thoughts and most of all I want him to be my friend and my not judge. I just feel lost and full of panic and pain. I am full of regret, guilt, and shame.

I think that the reason we can't fully, or even nearly comprehend Christ's Atonement is because we could not live with ourselves, or forgive ourselves for what we have done to Him. Maybe the reason we can't see our Heavenly Father when we pray or repent is because we couldn't and wouldn't live with ourselves if we saw His face break into sadness because of our actions? I think that the Lord may stay quiet when we have sinned because He doesn't want us to see or know how hurt He is?

A few days later, I continued to record my struggles:

I'm worried about myself. I don't feel strong. I don't feel able to defeat all temptation. I feel so guilty. If I was right spiritually then perhaps I wouldn't be so anxious and wake up with a sinking, nervous, sick feeling? I'm wavering badly. I'm becoming hard hearted and I'm afraid. I want to be living right. I feel like such a mess right now. I'm struggling to live the gospel. I lack enthusiasm and motivation. In the morning I'll pray and force myself to read.

This might sound like nonsense to you, and I know there are worse things in the world to be upset over, but I suppose all things are relative. My journals are just jam-packed with these self-deprecating entries:

Tonight I have felt so heavy at heart, such remorse of conscience for every sin I have committed. It's made me feel physically sick. I was a fool and I regret so much with all my soul for ever hurting my Saviour, and grieving the Spirit, and offending my Father. I am so sorry. I want the atonement to apply to me. I desire some assurance from God to help me know if I am okay or not. I want my garments to be clean. I want all sin to be burned from my soul, that I may stand blameless before God, that justice will have no claim. I fear the judgements to come, I fear in case the Lord is not pleased with me. I have been living the best I can now and been clean for 35 days now.

Another entry read as follows:

Today I have been really weighed down with all of my sins, inadequacies, mistakes, and foolish and wicked behaviour. I have committed so many iniquities. I am so imperfect and full of guilt. Satan has reminded me of all the things that I have done wrong, to the Lord, Kym, family, friends, and to myself. I feel sick and so heavy. I hate myself for my faults and for all the stupid errors I make. I can't escape. I'm so ashamed. Millions of my words, actions, thoughts, and intents stand against me. I fear judgement. I'm so scared that all of my sins are not blotted out, that I will be condemned. I worry that I hurt the Saviour too much. I worry what Heavenly Father is thinking about me right now. I pray and pray, but I still feel so unworthy for many years worth of crimes against God and others. I never feel safe that my transgressions are remembered no more. I fear, my heart is sorrowful, and I feel so alone. I feel like I've ruined everything. I sin, and sin, and sin, I HATE IT! I'm so sick to death of my weak nature. I have messed up so much and I don't know where to begin to make amends. How!? How can I have so great a testimony, how can I have such wonderful spiritual experiences, how can I have felt the Spirit burn within me and sanctify me, how can I love the gospel and God, and then mess it all up?

After reading my journals, I asked myself: Was I just mentally ill? Was there something unhinged in me that resulted in these mad ramblings? Why did I put myself through so much sorrow? Or should I just have kept the commandments like Mormons should and then all of this would have been avoided? I do not have the answers, but I wonder if there are other people out there putting themselves through this same hell because of religious brainwashing.

I am not sure if my friends felt the same magnitude of guilt that I did. I do not know why sin affected me so deeply. All I can put it down to is taking church doctrine as seriously as life and death.

I have seen the Church affect my friends in other ways though. One of my journal entries offers a small insight into how Tim was when he finished his missionary service:

He is merciful and wants to sort me out, i know that.
He is near and wanting to mold me into what he knows
i can be. I need to turn to him and trust in him.
Onething i really feel is that he will never give up on
me, he loves me so much and personally wants me
to repent so he can embrace me. What amazes me
is something i can't comprehend and that is that
the Saviour, even though i hurt him, upset him and
offend him... he looks past all that and still
reaches out to me. The main focus is not on my
sins but on the Love he feels for me, he views me
as a soul with a willing heart, not a foolish sinner.
I don't know why he does that, i hate myself for what
i do, but he has an unconditional Love. A few days
ago i felt so hard hearted and rebellious, but now
i feel softend and loved. The spirit is working in
me and leading me back to the Lord. Instead of
casting me off, he's bringing me back, he's the only
one who can clean me up and he's willing to do
it. Without Christ i'd be lost forever, i can't change
my past but Christ can undo the chains which bind
me. I want to be 100% Valiant.

A journal entry I wrote
on 6 September 2003.

For the last few nights Josh has stayed over. On Sunday night Tim came over
to stay. It was a great feeling having my best friends in the same room again.
Marcus came over too. We watched a DVD and just chilled. Tim seems unsettled
and a little stunned I think. I understand it must be hard adapting to home life
again. I was only away for a short while and when I came home I felt really
strange. Nothing quite felt the same, so two years away for Tim must be crazy.

I remember Tim being so shocked by an evening of TV. He could not believe
how raunchy commercial adverts were now, and how provocative music videos
seemed. He did not seem to enjoy the film we watched either. He really was
finding it hard to switch off his missionary brain.

Josh was also saying that he did not believe in the Church anymore. I knew he
was inactive, but I was surprised to hear that he did not even have a testimony
these days. This caused me great concern and I used to pray for him every night
that he would come back to the Lord.

I also found it difficult when Marcus decided to serve a mission. He was like
a younger brother to me and I was going to miss him badly. I knew the reality
of what a mission was and I feared for him. He was a recluse really and I did

not know how he would cope with mission life. I cried like a baby after I said goodbye to him at the airport. He was called to serve two years in Canada. He seemed to love his mission though, so maybe I had just projected my own fears onto him. When Marcus came home from his mission, he was told that his mum had left his dad and his whole world spun around. God was meant to bless missionary families. He had left his family behind, full of faith in God, and been rewarded with a broken home. Marcus does not go to church anymore, but he is happily married to a non-Mormon and living in South Korea.

Tim does not go to church either. The last time we spoke, he told me that he does not believe in it anymore. Josh's brother also served a two-year mission, but he has since left the Church after suffering a breakdown when he realised that it was all a lie.

Another one of my best friends, called Jesse, decided to get married instead of going on a mission. The bishop told him that he had chosen 'Plan B'. Needless to say, Jesse is another one of my friends who no longer associates with the Church.

After we all went through the same brainwashing and anointing process, the true miracle is that we all managed to escape the delusion and finally free our minds. Should I really have just kept quiet and left Mormonism alone after seeing the damage it caused to me and my loved ones?

18

History

On 1 September 2003, I returned to the States with Kym, my family, and our friend Danny. We had planned a two-week church history tour, where we would visit the first Mormon temple that Joseph Smith instructed to be built, the Smith's family home, and the Sacred Grove (where Joseph saw the First Vision).

On the third day of our trip, I proposed to Kym in the grounds of the Kirtland Temple in Ohio. I had wanted to ask her in the Grove, but I could not wait.

I recorded the following in my journal:

Kirtland Temple is beautiful. It's amazing standing by the great Temple where the Prophet Joseph Smith dwelt. The same sacred temple where the Prophet saw Angel Moroni, Elijah, and the Lord Jesus Christ. The early Saints were all around this area. Kym and I sat on a bench on the grounds, the temple was in view and beautifully lit, and the birds were singing. I asked Kym to walk with me around the temple, and then we went back to the bench. I asked Kym to sit down. I got down on one knee and asked my princess if she would marry me. I expressed my love for her and told her how beautiful she was. I held the ring box in my hand, still on my knee; I took it out and placed it on her finger. It fits! She cried and said 'yes!' We kissed and hugged. We are engaged!

The next day, we went back to Kirtland for the actual tour. I wrote that it 'feels different to what I expected. It's strange trying to connect with history'. The reason I included this is because this was how I felt about all of the church sites. I think I expected to feel the Spirit, or for these places to strengthen my testimony, but they did not. Even the Sacred Grove where the Heavenly Father and Jesus Christ were meant to have appeared just felt like being in any old ordinary woods.

The only place that did make me feel strange was Carthage Jail in Illinois because it is where Joseph Smith and his brother Hyrum were martyred. There were still bullet holes in the room and a recording that described their deaths. It was an eerie experience.

Kirtland Temple where I proposed to Kym. Ohio, September 2003.

At one of the church history sites, we saw a man with his two wives. He belonged to a break-off group of Mormons that continued to practice polygamy. This is where the confusion comes from. All throughout my church life, I was asked if my religion is the polygamous Mormon cult. When I was younger I was told, 'No, that's the reorganised church, not us', but when I became older and read about church History, I discovered that the early Saints did practice polygamy. Joseph Smith had multiple wives ranging from the ages of fourteen to fifty-six while he was prophet. The Church has said that some of these marriages were only 'for time and eternity', meaning a spiritual union that would seal them together in the next life. This could mean that some of his marriages were not necessarily a physical relationship on earth.

The fourteen-year-old girl that Joseph married was called Helen Kimball. She was the daughter of one of Joseph's close friends, Heber C. Kimball. By today's standards, this age seems shockingly perverse, but it would be unfair not to mention that it was legally acceptable for girls in their mid-teens to get married during this era. Many men in Joseph's inner priesthood circles also had multiple wives. The only thing I could never work out was why Joseph sealed other men's wives to himself—prophet privileges probably.

This controversial subject was never really discussed at church in my day, but when it was, members used to say that the reason the early Saints practised polygamy was because the women outnumbered the men as a result of Mormon persecution, and so the women needed priesthood holders to look after them and their children.

After Joseph Smith was killed, the Saints left Nauvoo, Illinois, because of heavy persecution and violence towards them. Brigham Young led the Saints on a painstaking journey to the Salt Lake Valley where the Lord had commanded the Saints to settle. When the Saints arrived in the Valley in 1847, at least 196 men and 521 women had entered into plural marriages. Brigham Young had over fifty wives.

It was not quite true for members to believe that polygamy resulted from the long pioneer voyage and persecution. I think this just made them feel better about it all. Joseph Smith informed his associates that he had been commanded by an angel three times between 1834 and 1842 to introduce plural marriage to the Saints. Apparently, he had tried to ignore this commandment because he knew that his own wife, Emma Smith, would not accept the doctrine and also because the practice was illegal. After his hesitation, Joseph reported that during the third appearance, the angel appeared with a drawn sword, threatening Joseph with destruction unless he went forward and obeyed the commandment.

I used to feel sympathy for Joseph's plight when I was a Mormon—poor Joseph, he really did not want to do this, did he? I suppose if Joseph was really restoring God's entire gospel back on earth, then he would have to bring back the doctrine which ancient prophets in the Old Testament practised.

Today I am more sceptical. Imagine I fancied having some more women in my life and I said to Kym, 'Babe, I've been commanded by God to get some more wives, and if I don't do it, an angel is going to run a fiery sword through me, so I guess I have to'. I do not think that would fly somehow. 'Oh well, looks like you're going to die then, darling' is what she would say. Unsurprisingly, Joseph's wife Emma had terrible problems with it. Many Saints also struggled with this doctrine. Some left the Church and others just refused to live it.

The spiritual purpose of plural marriage was basically so that more children could be born into the Church. Pre-earth life spirits could come down to bodies created in Mormon families and thus the Kingdom of God would flourish in the latter days.

In July 1843, while in Nauvoo, Illinois, Joseph Smith recorded the following revelation for the Saints. This is God speaking to Joseph, taken from Doctrine and Covenants Section 132:

> 4　For behold, I reveal unto you a new and an everlasting covenant; [plural marriage] and if ye abide not that covenant, then are ye damned; for no one can reject this covenant and be permitted to enter into my glory.

Want to go to heaven? Then you better keep this new commandment and start marrying some new wives. Yet what shall I tell the Mrs?

54 And I command mine handmaid, Emma Smith, to abide and cleave unto my servant Joseph, and to none else. But if she will not abide this commandment she shall be destroyed, saith the Lord; for I am the Lord thy God, and will destroy her if she abide not in my law.

Did you get that? You are to be exclusive to me while I am impregnating other women, and if you do not support this plan, then you will be destroyed. '60 Let no one, therefore, set on my servant Joseph; for I will justify him.' You should not attack me for this, God has my back.

61 And again, as pertaining to the law of the priesthood—if any man espouse a virgin, and desire to espouse another, and the first give her consent, and if he espouse the second, and they are virgins, and have vowed to no other man, then is he justified; he cannot commit adultery for they are given unto him; for he cannot commit adultery with that that belongeth unto him and to no one else.

Marrying two virgins is not cheating if they belong to me and no one else. '62 And if he have ten virgins given unto him by this law, he cannot commit adultery, for they belong to him, and they are given unto him; therefore is he justified.' Why stop at just two? How about ten? It is not adultery because they belong to me.

63 But if one or either of the ten virgins, after she is espoused, shall be with another man, she has committed adultery, and shall be destroyed; for they are given unto him to multiply and replenish the earth, according to my commandment, and to fulfil the promise which was given by my Father before the foundation of the world, and for their exaltation in the eternal worlds, that they may bear the souls of men; for herein is the work of my Father continued, that he may be glorified.

You ladies should not get any ideas though. If one of you hooks up with another dude, it is adultery and you will be destroyed. Do you not know that you were given to me to be baby-making machines?

Owing to much legal opposition from the Government, plural marriage faded out of the Church after the prophet Wilford Woodruff issued a manifesto in 1890, which put an end to the practice via God's command. Due to polygamy being illegal, the doctrine now hibernates. I used to believe that in the next life, I may be required to live it.

A form of plural marriage still exists in the Church today, but it is much more discreet because it is a spiritual union. When a man marries his wife in the temple, they are sealed together as husband and wife for time and all eternity.

This means there is no 'till death do us part'. Instead, they will continue their marriage in eternity. If a man's wife dies, and he marries another, he is permitted to also be sealed to his new bride for time and all eternity. So, in the next life, he would have two wives greeting him at the pearly gates. Yet here is another dash of Mormon misogyny: if the man dies, his wife is allowed to remarry, but not for time and all eternity.

We had an incredible two weeks in America, and I was glad to see where Joseph Smith had lived, where he had supposedly dug up the Gold Plates, and where the Book of Mormon was first published. I was disappointed that these places did not illuminate my soul though. I realised that no one would ever be converted by the Church History tour.

The best thing I learned while in Nauvoo was not anything religious, although it was about John Taylor, who became the Church's third prophet. I wrote about it in my journal:

> My favourite part of today was at John Taylor's home. We were told a great story about when the Saints had been forced into leaving Nauvoo because of the mobs. The Taylors moved West and after a few days of being there, one of John's sons was upset and crying. The boy finally told his father why he was distressed and it was because they had to leave behind a wooden rocking horse that John had made him. It was a beautiful, small horse, and the tail was made from John's own horse's hair. John had learned that his child had been praying about the rocking horse and this touched him. John Taylor, in disguise because of the mobs, rode all the way back to Nauvoo to collect the horse. He went through the backdoor and into the child's room and got the horse for his son. From then on, the horse remained with the Taylor family in Utah for years and years. Then when the Historic Nauvoo Sites were recently restored, the family wanted it returned to the child's original bedroom.

I thought this was a cool story, and as much as my feelings about the Church have soured, I cannot deny that the Saints suffered a lot at the hands of mobs for their beliefs.

Even though I was enjoying learning about church history, I could not escape from my guilt. How had it followed me all the way to Nauvoo? I could not even enjoy a vacation without it scratching away at me.

> When I get home I really want to make some changes. Sometimes I get so sick at the millions of sins I have committed. Satan loves to remind me about how much I've screwed up. He enjoys telling me how imperfect I am. There is no escape from it, and I can't change what I have done. It's a sorrowful state.
>
> Jesus Christ is my only hope. He is the only one who can save me and fix me. He is the only one who can forgive me and I desire with all my heart that He

would forgive and cleanse me. I've cried out for His help and mercy a lot today. I hope that my cries will be accepted soon. I want to be so valiant. I can be so much more. I don't want my Father in Heaven to be upset with me. I want to please Him, and to be so close to Him and my Lord. I miss them and it frightens me. I suppose this is the consequence of bad choices.

Today I was thinking about my mission. I just couldn't do it and I failed the Lord. I was so alone, so afraid, and anxious. I couldn't focus on the work; I just couldn't be a missionary. I pray to God that He will forgive me of my weakness. Maybe one day I will get the strength, ability, and chance to be a missionary again. Perhaps I'll be 'Elder Yeoman' again and show the Lord that I can make amends. Maybe I'll serve with Kym, or maybe I'll serve in the Spirit World.

There's something wrong with me. I feel like a hollow shell with too many chemicals crashing around inside. My heart feels like it's not there. I'm so empty. I feel inadequate and full of weakness. I've failed again and again. I despise myself for my behaviour. My temper rages like wildfire and my shame is unquenchable. My hands tremble and my body shakes. Anxiety controls me. I feel sick with panic. My chest is swelling and I feel nervous and nauseous. I hate it. I need air.

I was clearly still battling with panic attacks and depression. Maybe I should have sought out professional help again, although that had not worked for me before. I was not taking any medication or talking to anyone about how I was feeling at this point. My mental health troubles mixed with a heavy dose of religious guilt made for a vicious cocktail.

I really thought that there was no escape from this hell, but in 2005, my war with guilt would be history.

19

You Have No Power Here

Leading up to our wedding day, Kym and I decided to spend less time alone together and committed to staying strong for several months before we got married. We both wanted to be worthy for our temple marriage. Spiritually, we both felt great. We could not wait to be together, but we wanted to be free of guilt for our special day.

It is custom in church for your bishop to perform the wedding ceremony, but because of our bad history, I did not want my bishop to marry us. Instead, we asked the Stake President. This caused a little tension and awkwardness, but I do not think it was much of a surprise to him.

On 12 February 2005, Kym and I got married in Bracknell. The service went well and we had a great day with our friends and family. I had three best men at our wedding: my brother David, Tim, and Josh. Marcus was still serving his mission in Canada, but he sent an email to my dad to be read out during the speeches. My other best friend, Jesse, was there, and also a missionary who was currently serving in our ward whom my brother became best friends with. After our legal wedding, Kym and I travelled to the London Temple to be sealed together for time and all eternity.

Lots of friends came to support us but some of them had to wait outside in the freezing cold air because they were not considered 'worthy' to enter the sacred Mormon building. One of the missionaries who taught Kym the church discussions came along too. Funnily enough, he has also left the Church now. After we were sealed, Kym and I spent some time alone in the Temple's Celestial Room sitting under a sky blue-coloured ceiling with painted white clouds and lavish chandeliers hanging down. The Celestial Room is supposed to be a representation of Heaven. It was a special moment for us then, but when I look back, we would have felt just as posh sitting in a five-star hotel lobby. We then rushed off to the airport hotel and, the next day, flew to Paris for our honeymoon. Sex was officially legal for us, and there was absolutely no guilt that followed.

It is both fascinating and frightening to realise that my brain had been programmed to respond to sexual activity out of wedlock with guilt; equally, my

Right: Our wedding day,
12 February 2005.

Below: The London Temple

brain had been conditioned to respond to sexual activity within wedlock with joy—such is the power of religious brainwashing.

Was it all really as easy as flicking a switch on and off? Now that I was married, the switch had been flipped and the guilt was now deactivated. All those years of mental and emotional anguish were over in an instant. I never felt sexual guilt ever again; I had no need to. My prison sentence was over and I was a free man.

Can you believe that even when you are married, church leaders still have the nerve to stick their noses into your private business? To enter Latter-day Saint temples, a recommend is required. This is basically a temple pass, which lasts for two years. To acquire a temple recommend, you have two worthiness interviews: one with a member of the bishopric and another with a member of the stake presidency. The recommend expires after two years and so you have to repeat this process to renew it.

During these interviews, even if you are married, you are asked if you are keeping the law of chastity. You are not even fully free in marriage. Basically, they want to be sure that you are not being too adventurous or that you are not pressuring your partner, or involving pornography.

One leader started telling me how a man's sex drive can be higher and our wives may not always be in the mood, so you need to respect that. That poor bloke pretty much just confessed to me that he was not getting much action. I could not relate to any of it, so I felt a bit sorry for him when I left his office.

I was so glad that nothing affected me anymore. My sex life was between me and my wife. I always felt like King Théoden from *The Lord of the Rings* when leaders would try and nose in on my marriage. Mad laughter would accompany my desired response: 'You have no power here'.

Married life was awesome. I was finally happy because I had self-worth and felt pure for a change. There were no more demons laughing at me for masturbating and no devil rejoicing at my shame. There were no more nights spent begging God to forgive me because Kym had saved me. My prayers to God had never worked. I always fell back into temptation. My prayers for forgiveness never seemed to comfort me either. It turned out that my wife was the one to rescue me because the Church no longer possessed the control panel to my mind. I did not think like this back then though. I felt blessed. God had sent me Kym; all glory be to Him.

Check out the different tone in my journal too:

Kym and I are having the most amazing time in Cyprus! It is such a beautiful, paradisiacal island; we really are having a wonderful time. The beaches are so warm and smooth and the sea is refreshing and gorgeous. We're having a lot of fun.

I'm so in love with Kym. I thank the Lord for being so merciful and kind and blessing me with her. Our faith is strong, the Spirit is with us, and we are loving life.

As a married couple, Kym and I would often pray and study the gospel together. We became primary teachers and taught a class of young lads together every Sunday. We would often bear our testimonies at church, give talks, prepare Family Home Evenings, and join in with many other church activities. I was a diligent home teacher and I would help the missionaries whenever I could. In short, we were a solid Mormon couple and we enjoyed living our faith.

I had matured a lot as a person in marriage. I found a good balance between being spiritual and still enjoying myself. I never beat myself up about what movies I watched or what music I listened to. In my adult life, I realised that God was not as petty as Mormons made Him out to be. I could not see a supreme being with intelligence that we could not possibly fathom being hurt over my movie collection or my Metallica albums. He might be a bit offended by my Eminem CDs though, but surely even He could not deny Slim Shady's talents.

There was no way I had any time for nit-picking nonsense anymore. Does the creator of the universe really care if a missionary spikes his hair up a little? Does the Alpha and the Omega frown at a Mormon having a cheeky cup of coffee at work? Does the Saviour of the world shake His head in dismay if a young woman does not cover up her shoulders when she goes out with friends?

Why did God design my nutsack to fill up with sperm and then rebuke me when I needed it released? I cannot believe that it was considered more acceptable for me to cream my boxer shorts at night while having a provocative dream (which was usually way more graphic than anything else I would imagine) than it was to just release it like a normal person. I am sure it was more appropriate for my brother and I to have dealt with this issue privately, rather than have our boxers crusting away on our bedroom radiator some mornings before we sneaked them into the wash. It was not because we could have become addicted to porn either.

That reminds me, did Spencer W. Kimball really suggest that private masturbation could lead to me doing it with another male friend, and then us becoming gay? Let me check again in case I am mistaken. 'What is more, it (masturbation) too often leads to grievous sin, even to that sin against nature, homosexuality. For, done in private, it evolves often into mutual masturbation—practiced with another person of the same sex and thence into total homosexuality'. No, I was right, that was what he said. Let me tell you, Mr Kimball, in all my years of private masturbation, not once did I think, 'you know what might change it up? I'll get Josh over for a double whammy'. All right that's enough about all that, though I am not sure I can ignore the homophobia.

I am ashamed to say that growing up Mormon, I was homophobic, not because I was scared or threatened by homosexuality, but because I was taught that it was an unnatural sin in the eyes of God. In fact, the sin was so serious that God turned the Old Testament's equivalent of San Francisco into ashes. The gays were so perverse in Sodom and Gomorrah that they even tried it on with angels of the Lord. Holy shocking shenanigans, Batman.

Back in the eighties and nineties, every Mormon I knew would have said that homosexual behaviour was of the devil and unacceptable in society. It was seen as heinous in and out of the Church in those days. My school peers would use gay slurs as insults and I did not know anyone that was openly gay either. My understanding as a Mormon was that being gay was a choice, a temptation from Satan, abhorrent in the eyes of the Lord.

I was in my thirties when I began to change my mind. I realised that my opinions of the LGBTQ community were not my own, but what the Church taught. What right did I have to judge anyone else? I really did not care who wanted to be with whom. 'Live and let live' became my new motto, providing no one was getting hurt.

The internet really opened my eyes up to alternative lifestyles and gave me knowledge that thankfully changed my ignorant views. I was never anti-gay or involved in any crusades to stop gay marriage, but I did view being gay as a sin against God.

I have a good friend who is bisexual and ex-Mormon. For all the years she was active, she suppressed her true sexuality and felt afraid of being open about it. My MTC friend Elder Kent has also come out as bisexual since leaving the Church.

I have another friend who served a mission for seven months while hiding his homosexuality. He was put on medication for panic attacks, which made him a zombie, until he finally went home. He told me, 'When I came home early, my mission was considered a complete failure; it really would have been easier on my family had I been killed. The experience was unbelievable. It took me and my family years to recover, but we never viewed the Church the same again'. He has been happily married to his husband for twenty years now and has been fortunate to have the support of his family. There are many people out there who are not so lucky and end up being disowned by their own.

The Church's public relations face has changed since the dark ages of no internet. It very much has the attitude now of 'love the sinner, but not the sin'. People would have been excommunicated in the eighties for being gay, but the Church would not get away with that now. I believe the internet has made the Church tread more carefully.

Today, church leaders express their love for its gay members, providing that they do not act on their gay tendencies. For the life of me, I cannot imagine how anyone that is gay would want to be associated with the Church, but it is probably more complicated for them than I can understand. If they have a testimony of the Church, then what else can they do but respect its doctrines?

Something I have noticed in recent times is a rise in gay Mormon support groups, which are full of active members trying to make doctrinal changes from within. I applaud them for their efforts and I know that these support networks help people all over the world.

The pessimist in me knows that the Church will probably never change its stance on homosexuality. It will continue to offer support and half-hearted understanding, but if it ever gave equal rights to its gay membership, then it would in turn discredit hundreds of years of doctrine and make itself look like one big fraud, not that it needs much help with that.

Something else the internet exposed which the Church had to officially acknowledge is that there are several accounts of Joseph Smith's First Vision, and not just one like the Church had led everyone to believe for decades.

Joseph's first handwritten account in 1832 explains that the main reason he prayed in the Grove was not to find out which religion was true but because he was feeling guilt for his sins and desired forgiveness. This account does not mention any opposition from Satan as he prayed; neither does it mention two personages. This account only has Christ appearing to him to forgive him of his sins. The 1835 account says that one divine personage appeared, followed by another, as well as many angels. The 1838 account does not mention any angels. The latter account is the one I included at the beginning of this book, which is the one the Church teaches as canon.

The discrepancies in these various accounts shook up a lot of members that I know. Some were wobbled by them and others ignored them because of their testimonies. Personally, I find it astounding that such a monumental event like the First Vision would need altering at all, no matter how small the differences. Surely, you could not forget the details of something like that? I smiled to myself when I learned that Mormonism spawned from guilt—how apt.

It has also come to light that Joseph Smith translated the Book of Mormon by looking into a hat at a 'seer stone' to translate the record. Apparently, when he would look into the hat words would appear on the stone and his scribe would write them down. What is the point of even having the Gold Plates if the words just appear on the stone anyway? It sounds bonkers to me.

20

The Final Nail

My past experiences and my new-found guilt-free lifestyle had made me a much more rounded person. I felt like I could help people much more now that I was out of the woods and basking in the sunlight.

As a home teacher, I really began to care about the families I would visit and I became more compassionate rather than judgemental if people struggled. I would often listen to people's troubles and do my best to offer them spiritual guidance. Grown men, sometimes older than me, felt the need to confess their sins of masturbation to me, and for the first time in my life, I realised how unnecessary that was. Now my own guilt had been switched off, I felt so much empathy for people who reminded me of my old self. I told one guy to just do his best and if he slipped up then it was not a big deal. 'You don't need to tell me or the bishop about it, buddy, just pray and try again'—how I wished that someone had just said that to me.

Sometimes, people would need priesthood blessings from me, whether it was for illness, exams, job interviews, or just to be comforted. I performed tons of them over the years. I was confident in my ability as a priesthood holder and I felt genuine love and concern for people. It was a great feeling to serve others instead of being trapped in my own head for a change.

Occasionally, I would encounter some tough situations as a home teacher. My friend James, who I used to knock doors with before my mission, had a really bad problem with smoking weed. Just like I had battled back and forth with immorality, he had been battling with the Word of Wisdom for the whole of his church life. In the end, he became really messed up mentally. I know it was a combination of drugs and indoctrination, but he just did not feel capable of meeting Mormon standards and so he gave up. I used to be so tight with him, but we drifted over the years when he became really anti-Mormon and found his own version of God. I felt sad that he did not get the attention or help he needed because he was one of the best people I knew at church.

It was sad seeing how people could be affected by religion. Another good friend of mine was inactive for the best part of his teenage life but came back out in his twenties. He went absolutely nuts when he came back to church. He was overzealous in a lethargic ward and I knew it would only be a matter of time before he would burn out. When I last spoke to him, he told me that he hated the Church now and was unhappy in his marriage. He said the only reason he got married in the first place was because his bishop had told him to in a blessing.

One of my friends split up from his wife because he abused his power as a priesthood holder. He took his role as patriarch in the home too far and became a dictator to his household. His wife kicked him out and wanted a divorce, and he became mentally unstable. This couple had been separated and living apart for ages, yet he would still demand sex from her because they were technically still sealed together by temple marriage. Priesthood authority can be a dangerous power in the wrong hands. I used to really like this guy when he first came on the scene, but indoctrination ruined him.

There are some lovely members of the Church. Many of them have great hearts and do a lot of good in the world, but equally, there are some real self-important, judgemental assholes who take their roles far too seriously. I suppose such is the case in all walks of life.

Now I had Kym as my wife, I felt so much better about attending church. My mission stigma still hung around in the background, but I felt like I had reinvented myself and people started to accept me again. I was productive in my church callings; I would bless the sacrament, give talks, and bear testimony in many meetings. No one could refute my spiritual confidence; not even past guilt could destroy my peace of mind.

Some people in the ward did not really like my family. We were too outspoken and perhaps my mission experience had tainted our image. I seemed to be out of the firing line now that I was married and seen to be doing everything required of me, but my younger brother took some flak.

One night, a young woman and her friend got stranded somewhere and they called my brother, David, up and asked if he would mind picking them up. It was late, but he went out and took them home. The next day, the mother of one of the young women phoned my dad up, raging at David for doing it. 'That won't be happening again! How inappropriate for him to have my daughter in his car!' We could not believe that she was attacking David for not leaving her daughter stranded somewhere in the middle of the night.

Another time, a new lad from Canada moved into the ward and became friends with David. The family who was looking after this lad told him not to hang around with my brother because he was a troublemaker and a bad influence. When David began seeing a church girl in his late teens, someone took her aside and told her that she should not date him because he was not worthy of her because he was not a returned missionary, so she stopped seeing him.

So many pathetic little incidents like this happened to him. He once said 'crap' in a chapel and a member of the stake presidency reprimanded him in front of everyone.

Other than these irritating incidents, my family remained strong and we continued to enjoy our lives in the gospel. I remember that during this time, my brother and our friend Jesse would spend hours and hours discussing the deeper doctrines and mysterious of the gospel. We would stay up until about 3 a.m. chatting or going into the woods to pray together. We laugh about it now. An owl would hoot and we would panic and think it was the Devil trying to put us off. We also used to try and outdo each other's prayers by speaking like we were prophets of old and trying to sound really clever. We used to talk about how we would all end up as bishops or stake presidents. One bishop told me that he believed that I would end up as a general authority; I must look like such a let-down to him now.

A few years into our marriage, Kym and I began to talk about trying for a baby. I was reluctant at first because we were paying a ridiculous amount of rent for a one-bedroom flat. I was also aware that my anxiety disorder was still a burden to me and the stress might unleash a wave of panic attacks. I did not feel like I was financially stable enough either, so we agreed that maybe it was not the best time for us to start trying.

Not long after these early discussions, I attended a friend's sealing at the Temple. While I was there watching my friend be sealed to his wife for time and all eternity, I felt a spiritual prompting telling me that the Lord wanted me to have a child. I felt like my heart was bursting with warmth and love and I promised God that I would despite my aforementioned worries. The next day, I sat Kym down and told her about my spiritual experience in the Temple. She was so excited. We hugged and then thanked the Lord in prayer for giving us this revelation. My worries vanished and I felt confident that the Lord knew best and that he would bless us to be able to get by. I was so happy that I told my family that we were trying for a baby.

It was all Kym and I could talk about together. We were so happy to be embarking on this new adventure. It felt so right and so we got to work. After several months of trying, we began to feel a little disappointed that we had not yet fallen pregnant, but it was early days so we would just be patient and trust in God. He knew when the time would be right for us.

A year and a half passed by before we fell pregnant. I was shovelling snow out of the driveway of our new house one evening when suddenly Kym swung the door open and said that she just took a pregnancy test. 'We're pregnant!' I could not believe it. I did not even know she was taking a test. I dropped the shovel and ran over to her and hugged her tight. This was the happiest moment of our lives. We were going to have a baby.

We could not contain our excitement, so we announced the news to our family and a couple of close friends who knew that we had been trying. The Lord did know when the time was right after all. We were no longer living in our cramped flat; we had just taken out a mortgage on a new house and now, after such a long time, we had fallen pregnant.

After a few days on cloud nine, I decided that I needed to give Kym a priesthood blessing. Kym sat down in a chair in our home and I laid my hands gently on top of her head. 'Kym Yeoman, by the authority of the Melchizedek Priesthood which I hold, and in the name of Jesus Christ I lay my hands upon your head to give you a blessing'.

I paused to wait for divine inspiration. When I felt as if the Spirit was flowing through my veins, I began to speak. I cannot remember the exact words I spoke, but I know that I blessed her to be healthy and well during her pregnancy. I blessed our baby to be strong and healthy, and to get to us safely. I blessed my wife with everything she stood in need of and poured the love of God into her heart. During the blessing, I felt that our baby was going to be a boy. I almost announced the sex but decided not to just in case I was wrong, so instead I just blessed 'our baby'. After the blessing, we felt full of love. I told Kym that I thought we were going to have a boy and if we did, I would like to call him Caden James Yeoman. We started to refer to the baby as 'he'.

When the time arrived for our first scan, Dad dropped us off at the hospital and we went to the gynaecology ward to see our baby for the first time. We were so excited. The nurse laid Kym down on the bed, put some gel on her belly, and turned the screen to face us. As she scanned Kym's womb, our hearts sank. All we could see was a black screen. The nurse said that she could not detect a heartbeat. She then told us to wait where we were and she left the room. Kym started to cry and started shaking her head at me in disbelief. The nurse came back into the room and apologised to us. 'I'm sorry, you've miscarried'. Our hearts cracked into pieces and the room began to spin. I could not believe it. We left the hospital and I called Dad to come and get us. I felt stunned. I sat in the backseat of the car, trying to fight back the tears that were already rolling down my cheeks. I wanted to be strong for Kym and I did not want to break down, so I bit my lip and tried to hold myself together.

We got out of the car and walked into the house in silence. We were both shell-shocked. I cannot remember anything else about that day other than our house phone ringing and ringing while we hid ourselves away in our bedroom.

A few days later, Kym was bleeding heavily so we went to the hospital. No one was really concerned about it. This was all apparently part of a miscarriage, so we went home in the early hours of the morning. The next day, Kym and I got up and went for lunch in a local café. My friend Josh had given us a card with £100 inside to go out for the day with. He thought we should try and take our minds off of things. We had planned to spend the afternoon in Guildford, but Kym started to experience intense pain. We came home and I called my dad to ask if he could come and help us. Dad gave Kym a priesthood blessing, but soon after, Kym bent over in agony and just started screaming. We called an ambulance and the paramedics gave her gas and air. I got in the ambulance with her and she became a little delirious on the gas and air but that was better than hearing her scream out in pain. When we got to the hospital, Kym was given morphine, paracetamol, and more gas and air. She was screaming so much that she tore a small hole in a lung, which caused an air bubble to get trapped outside. Someone came in and rushed her off to somewhere else in the hospital and I remember just sitting in this small room sobbing. I hated seeing my wife suffer like this. We spent hours in that little room. Kym was in pain but also high as a kite. She kept telling me to suck in some gas and air for fun.

We eventually came home in the early hours of the morning and slept. I remember lying next to Kym and pleading with the Lord to let this nightmare end. I prayed that Kym's pain would cease and that she would be okay.

Later that day, the pain returned and the screaming began. I phoned my brother and he came and picked us up and drove us to A&E. We sat in A&E for ages while Kym was doubled over in pain, screaming the place down. The receptionists were distraught by her screaming and eventually just got me a wheelchair to put her in and she received treatment. The doctor wanted to keep Kym in for the night, so I came home. We had no idea what was going on. No one was really explaining anything to us and we were feeling traumatised by this whole ordeal. I walked into an empty house that night and just cried myself to sleep. I was not even thinking about the miscarriage anymore; I just hated seeing Kym in so much pain. At about 5 a.m., Kym phoned me up and asked me to come and get her. She was really upset because she had finally passed the placenta and pregnancy sack and it broke her heart all over again.

We were told before Kym left that her body had essentially gone into labour to pass the placenta and sack, which had caused her such horrendous pain. Finally, her physical suffering was over, but emotionally, she was wrecked.

When we got home, a Sister from church came to see us. I had updated my social media, so she was aware of the situation. She was not close to us at all. I had barely spoken to her, but here she was in our living room, telling us she had been through five miscarriages. I am sorry that she had been through that, but she also had children too, and it felt like she was belittling our grief by outdoing it with hers. Several people wanted to talk to us about their miscarriages too, but it was the last thing we wanted to hear. We just wanted to be left alone.

The day after Kym was out of hospital, her Visiting Teacher knocked on the door to see her. I was watching football in the living room with my friends, so she did not come in. When Kym closed the door, she told me that this woman had pretty much said to her, 'It's important to try and look forward now and try and move on from your grief. Look what happened to Lots' wife when she looked back to Sodom and Gomorrah; she turned into a pillar of salt. It's your duty to keep trying to bear God's children, so don't give up'.

Kym had only been home from hospital for a day and already, she was being told to 'get over it'. Kym phoned up the Relief Society President and told her that she never wanted a visit from that woman again.

We kept to ourselves for a little while and I became really protective of Kym. I asked people to stop trying to help her because it was only making things worse. At church, someone thought it would be a good idea to put a new born baby in Kym's arms to try and help her. It seemed like everything was just salt in the wound. During a Sunday school lesson, the teacher started reading a scripture about the pains of childbirth as a joke to one of the Sisters who had just been through labour. Kym got upset and walked out and I followed her. That was the last time we went to church.

Our miscarriage caused us immense grief. At first, all we thought about was the physical pain that Kym had gone through. It was very traumatic for her and she began having night terrors. The emotional anguish came later. We felt devastated that we had lost our baby. People would try and belittle our miscarriage by saying that it was not really a baby yet because it was so early on, but it was to us. We had bought baby clothes and I had even mentally named him. Our joy was now our misery and we could not cope with the loss.

It was too hard to attend a church that was so family orientated. It was a slap in the face to listen to talks or to read scriptures about 'multiplying and replenishing the earth' with children. Our ward was heaving with kids. During this period, most of our close friends also started to have babies and we found it all too difficult to bear. We could not understand how God had allowed this to happen to us. No one had any answers.

People would try and get us back out to church, but even the pushiest leaders did not have anything left to say to us when we explained that it was just too painful for us to be there. We could not be around pregnant people or people with newborns for a while. We could not stomach hearing talks about procreating and raising children in the gospel. I am sure people thought we were selfish and self-centred, but we had to protect ourselves. Some people would try and tell us that there were other people out there who have had worse experiences than us. I know there are, but it is all relative, is it not? This was our pain, and this was how we were dealing with it.

We decided that we would go back to church when we fell pregnant again. As soon as Kym felt better, we started trying again. My dad and I gave Kym several blessings, telling her that we would again fall pregnant and have a baby. Even though I did not go out to church, I was still praying and putting my faith and trust in the Lord.

Kym became severely depressed after the miscarriage and we started to get really frustrated and angry that we were not falling pregnant again. For a few months, we were a great support to each other, but we began to cope with it in different ways. Kym needed to talk about it while I closed up and did not want to talk about it anymore. I remember sitting downstairs on my Xbox trying to distract my mind most evenings while Kym would be tucked away in bed crying. Our house felt so empty while we each dealt with our own depressions in our own ways. We remained close and we were still trying for a baby; it was just that we got to a point where we could not help each other with the grief anymore.

Another year went by and more of our friends started having kids. The following year, my brother and his wife also had a baby. We never felt resentful, quite the opposite—we were happy for all of our friends and family, and we love their children, but every now and then we would get home, go to bed, and feel sadness. Why was God not blessing us yet?

Everyone had some theory. 'Your baby might have been too precious for this world'. 'You'll see your baby in the next life'. 'I'm sure the same Spirit will come down next time you get pregnant'. Sometimes, I wished people would say, 'I know it's shit. I'm sorry for what you're going through'.

The longer we stayed inactive, the more people became frustrated that we were not moving on from it. People started to overstep too. 'I think if you want God to bless you, you need to put yourselves in a position for Him to bless you'. 'If you start praying and reading your scriptures, you'll start getting blessed'.

Everyone was driving me crazy. Is that how it works? You have to earn it? Well, how does that apply to people that get knocked up from a one-night stand? I doubt those deadbeat parents on chat shows were praying and reading their scriptures before they had sex. Why does the Lord send spirits down to them and not to good people like us?

Nothing anybody had to say helped. If people had to walk on eggshells around us, then that was their problem; they simply should not come near us.

My sadness was starting to transform into anger. Had people just left us alone to spiritually hibernate while we tried for another baby, I may have ended up going back out to Church eventually. Yet when people started to push me into turning back to God, I started to push back.

During this defensive state of mind, I began to realise the reasons why I was not turning back to God. Why should I? It was His fault that I was inactive in the first place. He had not answered any of my prayers. It had been years now. I thought God could walk on water, cure the blind, and raise the dead. Why could He not bless us with a baby? Why should I have to start sucking up to Him again? If He wanted me back, He could come to me.

I was mad at God, but then I had been mad at Him before. He had abandoned me as a missionary, and now He was abandoning me in my marriage. The biggest kick in the teeth though was when I realised that it was His Spirit that had given me the revelation to start trying for a baby in the Temple in the first place. Then, a year and a half went by to try our faith, but we endured and finally conceived, but then we were repaid with loss. I did not understand any of it.

Among my grief and depression, I had forgotten that I was giving Kym a priesthood blessing and feeling inspired to bless her and my child with health and strength when, in reality, she would have already miscarried by then. We worked out the timing, and we had lost our baby when I was 'feeling' that it was a boy. When I connected these dots, the final nail was hammered into the coffin and for the first time in all of my life, I honestly lost my faith. That blessing had felt so inspired, almost like divine revelation, and yet it was all meaningless— what a cruel trick. I vowed that I would never give another priesthood blessing again.

I no longer had any faith in the priesthood. I realised that I could no longer trust my feelings. They had been proven as an unreliable source for truth.

When I thought about it in more depth, I knew that all of my beliefs were based solely on feelings; the warm fuzzies could not be trusted anymore. What did I actually know for certain? Well, I knew that I could not trust in priesthood blessings, nor could I trust in my emotive interpretation of 'the Spirit'.

My mind was reeling. Had I just been conjuring up my spiritual experiences all along? My brain was conditioned to think that if I prayed or read scripture, I would feel warmth and love. My brain was indoctrinated to respond to sin with feelings of guilt. My brain was programmed to feel 'the Spirit' if I uttered mantras like, 'By the authority of the Holy Melchizedek priesthood'. I may as well have said 'By the power of Greyskull, I have the power!' for all the good it did.

I started to think about priesthood blessings and how useful they actually were. Most of the time, people needed comfort, faith, or help getting over a cold. If someone needs comfort and there is a priesthood holder spilling out positive affirmations, then they are going to feel uplifted. If someone needs a faith injection and a priesthood holder tells them what they secretly want to hear, then they are going to take heart in his words. If someone wants help getting over a cold, then a blessing would be given, but did it ever really speed up the recovery time for anyone? No. If someone wanted to pass a driving test and they had a blessing, there was a one-in-two chance of them succeeding. If they did pass, then it was a miracle and the blessing worked. If they did not, then perhaps someone's faith was not strong enough, maybe next time.

I reflected on the more serious blessings I had encountered too. I remember before my mission, I was asked by a bishop to assist in a blessing that a man asked for to cure his deformed hand. He was told that if he had faith, and we had faith, then God could heal him through the priesthood. I came away from that blessing feeling sorry for him because the blessing was awkward and vague. I think he had a few blessings after this one but none of them made any difference to his hand. I always thought it cruel to give him hope like that.

After our miscarriage, a close family friend was diagnosed with cancer. My dad blessed her that she would be cured of it, but shortly after, the cancer spread. He also gave her a blessing that she would be comforted towards the end, but before she died, she suffered a painful death and Dad witnessed it. Dad also lost his faith in priesthood blessings after that and has never given one since.

I also recall another Sister in our stake that was diagnosed with cancer and told through a priesthood blessing that she would be cured, but she never was—

how awful to give her loved ones hope like that. I am certain the priesthood holder believed it, but it was his willpower trying to heal her, not God's.

I have never witnessed firsthand, or known anyone who has been miraculously blessed by the priesthood. Most blessings are usually small time, with a fifty-fifty success rate. It is just like prayers; there is a one-in-two chance of something going the way you want it to.

When my faith in blessings died, I then questioned the priesthood itself. Did any of us really have any authority to act in God's name? I felt like such a gullible fool. I had no power. Belonging to the priesthood was like belonging to a really rubbish version of Hogwarts School of Witchcraft and Wizardry, only the spells I had learned were not as reliable.

To begin with, I did not question anything else about the Church. I just knew that I did not trust or have any faith left in the priesthood. It had let me down and hurt my wife. I was done with it all. There would be no more blessings.

I lost confidence in myself as a person. I had always relied on being a priesthood holder. I took pride in it, and now I was as lost as a leaf in the wind. I needed to take some timeout and to be left alone, but people just cannot help themselves, can they? On one occasion, I received a random phone call from a man in our ward. He was not even in a leadership position, but he had the audacity to say: 'You need to come back to church and you need to support your wife'. He went further with his unwelcomed criticisms of my life too: 'You need to go back to college and get some new grades, and be a better support to Kym'. Who the hell did he think he was? I barely even knew this guy, and here he was on the phone telling me how to improve myself and what I should be doing for my wife whom he did not even know? I wish I could say this was an isolated incident, but it was not. When I was suffering with severe anxiety and depression, some clown in the ward told Kym to 'kick me into shape and make me get a job'.

I did not miss seeing these prying prats when I left, and as time moved on, I did not think about the Church anymore. I asked the current bishop to stop any members or leaders from visiting us and my family respected that I did not want to go back out to church. Kym and I just wanted to try and rebuild ourselves, but it was a slow process.

My dad brought joy back into our lives one evening when he knocked on the door and delivered a gorgeous terrier puppy called Tilly to us. It took us by surprise and we were not sure we were ready for a dog. As soon as we cuddled her, we fell in love and Kym looked at me and said, 'I want her'.

Tilly brought so much happiness back into our home. Her naughty but lovable ways really changed the vibe in our house. We ended up getting a second dog to keep her company, a Patterdale terrier called Lincoln. I suppose only dog lovers will truly understand this, but these two furry little delights saved us from falling deeper into despair.

Occasionally, over the next few years, I would have discussions with my brother and Jesse about my lack of faith in the priesthood and my anger at God. As we talked about church doctrine, I began to notice that I was not really onboard with much of it anymore. I would come home from each discussion and just think to myself, 'You know what? I don't believe that anymore. What a load of crap'.

At one point, my brother was trying vigorously to get himself as near to perfection as he possibly could as a Mormon. He was very much like I was the year before my mission. He was praying all the time, fasting, and reading scripture and other church literature. He became really interested in people's near-death experiences and fascinated by the afterlife. He was serving in a church calling and trying everything he could to try and make a difference in his ward, but he soon became demoralised by the apathy of those he was working with. He finally burned out after trying so hard to get close to God and to understand the mysteries of the universe. I felt sympathy for him as I watched him trying to obtain answers to his questions. He was like me when I was young, hoping to see an angel, or hoping the Lord would grant him a vision to better understand the eternal plan. It was another reminder of how frustratingly tormenting religion can be for people. You invest your heart and soul into it and are rewarded with silence from above.

The more I spoke with David and Jesse about their struggles and their opinions, the more I began to be vocal about my own views. It was strange for all three of us to hear me say that I did not know if the Church was true anymore. I was not even sure I believed in God.

Line upon line, precept upon precept, my testimony started to peel away like an apple skin until there was nothing left but a rotting core.

21

Aftermath

When I was thirty, I had my first alcoholic drink. One afternoon, I randomly decided that I needed to have the experience of tasting the 'strong stuff'. Why was I keeping the Word of Wisdom now that I did not believe that the Church was true? I went out to a local store and purchased a small bottle of Jack Daniel's whiskey. I wanted to do it right, so I also purchased a whiskey glass. I wanted to feel moody, like a beaten down detective in a film noir drowning his sorrows with a Jack in a gloomy rundown bar. I had no idea how alcohol would affect me though, so I decided to try it in my kitchen at home, even though that scene is not as cool. I poured some in a glass and downed it neat—holy hell, that burned. I liked it though and was surprised that I did not feel any different. So, I thought I would try it again, but with some ice this time; that was better. A few seconds later, I was feeling wobbly, so I sat down on a chair, feeling like a man—a dizzy man, but still.

A little angel, which I like to call twenty-seven years of Mormon indoctrination, tried to whisper something in my ear but I flicked it away like an irritating fly. I was not going to let old habits govern my choices anymore. The little devil on my shoulder won this round. This was the process I went through for a while. Even though I had lost my testimony, I could not undo all those years of Mormon thinking just like that.

I soon discovered that the more I fought through the conditioning, the easier it became. It took ages for me to allow anyone to post a photo of me with a beer on social media because I knew that people would get weird about it. I eventually pushed through that apprehension and decided people would just have to deal with my lifestyle now. I was not encroaching on anyone's beliefs, but I was not going to hide away like a naughty teenager in adulthood. I know judgements were made and people got touchy because my interaction with members suddenly dipped.

My family were still attending church and our inactivity troubled them, not because they were disapproving or offended that I had the odd beer every now and then, but because they were concerned about the welfare of my soul. We never fell out over it, but it was a sensitive time for everyone. We did not want to hear anything of a spiritual nature and they were hoping that we would return to our faith, so it was a fine balance to keep everyone content.

Kym and I were still facing fertility problems. We had learned that the easiest way to cope with the frustration was to not build our hopes up anymore. It was horrid to be so up and down all the time. Sometimes, Kym would be late and so our hopes would rise, but a pregnancy test would always bring them back down. This scenario happened more times than I can count. We settled on having no hope and just getting on with our lives. At least then, we would not be disappointed. If we did conceive then it would be an amazing surprise without all of the ups and downs. This approach is not for everybody, but it helped us get by. It was tiresome to have people telling us that if we came back to church, we would be in a better position for the Lord to bless us. 'It will happen for you soon, I've put you on the Temple prayer roll'. That was not helpful either.

Wishful comments and prayers did not influence anything. Seven years passed and Kym began to suffer with pains caused by endometriosis, which resulted in her having an operation. A specialist at the hospital then told us that because she suffers with endometriosis, there is a high risk of ectopic pregnancy, so in order to be safe and hopefully prevent further operations, it was advised that contraceptive measures be put in place. We decided that Kym's health had to take priority and after many discussions, we agreed that we would have to stop trying for a baby. The emotional strain became too much for us and we knew that we would not be able to cope with possibly going through another miscarriage or having IVF treatment fail.

Despite us telling the bishop that we did not want any official visits from the Church, two new missionaries knocked on our door one evening. We told them we had asked not to have any visits and they said that they had not been briefed on that. They seemed like good lads, so we let them in for a quick chat and a drink. I felt sympathy for missionaries because I knew firsthand how intense their days were, so we said if they ever wanted a short break from 'the work' they were welcome to come and have dinner here providing they respected our wishes about not speaking about the gospel. They agreed, and so they began to visit us every so often. They were nice guys, but I instantly saw through their tactics. First it was, 'Can we just pray before we leave?'; then, it was, 'Can we just read you a scripture?'; and then it was, 'Can we challenge you to start reading The Book of Mormon again?' I felt a little annoyed in the end because they seemed to like us and care about us, but it was all dependant on whether we would come back to church. We stopped the visits and learned our lesson—no more missionaries were coming in, no matter how genuine they seemed.

I spent six years inactive before I began to voice my opinions about my church experiences online. I was always very sensitive and respectful to my Mormon friends, so I never came out guns blazing. Little things started to grate on me at

Me and Kym in July
2016.

first. I felt annoyed by double standards. Some Mormons felt it appropriate to
approach me with their missionary-minded reactivation attempts, or with their
uncompromising opinions, but then could not accept my counteractive opinions
in return. How is it not hypocritical for people to try and persuade me to come
around to their Mormon way of thinking, but then take offence when I try and
persuade them with my non-Mormon thinking? I have heard, 'It's insulting to
criticise and mock my sacred beliefs'. However, it is okay for them to insult me
by judging me and telling me I need to repent unless I want to spend eternity in
Hell? That is pretty rude to be honest.

Recently, my whole family went inactive and people just could not help
weighing in about it. My dad became more vocal than me on social media and
he received a lot of flak for it. We have had members of the Church that we have
known for decades blank us in public, and my parents have been dropped like a
bad habit by people they classed as friends.

Even though Kym and I had not attended church for six years, we were still
technically members. We had a discussion and concluded that we no longer
wanted to associate ourselves with a religion that we no longer believed in or
supported. I did not want to be connected to a church that caused me so much

mental and emotional damage over the years. I did not want to be part of a church that has a history of racism, and is still misogynistic and homophobic in 2017. I also wanted to be able to speak freely without facing church disciplinary action. I am sure that I am viewed as an apostate now, especially after writing this book, and so technically, the Church could have excommunicated me. I would not want to be discussed in any judgemental way by leaders who still held the power over my membership. It would have been humiliating to have two priesthood holders knock on my door one day and hand me a letter of excommunication. There was no way I wanted them to have that satisfaction after all the hurt I had been through growing up and as a missionary. At least I had the power to decide my fate, and I chose to leave.

The current bishop of my local ward is a good man. He has always shown compassion and friendship to us and even admitted his understanding to some of our problems with Mormonism. Before Christmas 2016, the bishop came to our home to collect all of our Latter-day Saint books, which we were donating to the ward. Kym handed the bishop an envelope with our resignation letters in and he thanked us. It was a bit awkward because we realised that he thought we were giving him a Christmas card. 'You probably don't want to thank us for that,' Kym said, and the bishop realised what was inside the envelope. I helped carry the boxes of books to his car and we spent about twenty minutes talking. He was really sympathetic and respectful, and I appreciate how easy he made the whole process. The bishop contacted us a few days later and said that our names had disappeared from the Church's records. We were officially no longer members of The Church of Jesus Christ of Latter-day Saints.

For about ten seconds, I felt strange, almost sad, but then I got over it. The weight of Mormonism had finally been lifted off of my back and I felt liberated. I cannot express how happy I felt knowing that I had escaped religious delusion.

After twenty-seven years of brainwashing the odds of me ever being able to escape it were slim. I was never just a casual member of the Church either; I took everything literally and to heart, but I had finally done it. I was out and I was free. I began a process of trying to reprogram my mind back to its default settings. My thoughts were no longer influenced by Mormonism; I could make my own mind up now. I could start thinking for myself.

In the early morning hours of the 10 July 2016, I sat at my computer and began to vent about my experiences with Mormonism. I knew that some people had been wondering why I had taken the drastic measure of getting my name removed because this would break my temple covenants and temple marriage, invalidate my priesthood, and if I ever wanted to return to Church, I would have to be re-baptised. I felt the need to finally give my reasons now that I was ex-Mormon and could not be held accountable by the Church for speaking out against it. I linked the blog to my Facebook page and went to sleep after wondering if I should have expressed myself so openly. When I awoke the next day and saw a flood of supportive messages, I was relieved. I thought that would be the last thing I ever said about the Church. It felt good to unburden myself, but it was even better to hear that my blog had resonated with several other 'less active' members of the Church.

Most of the people that offered me support or were kind enough to read the post were non-Mormons. I was actually quite surprised by their interest, and equally as surprised by the silence I received from members of the Church who I counted as friends. I expected a dialogue, rather than a backlash, but we still seem to be on radio silence. I have realised how incredibly tense it is when there is a religious elephant in the room. It baffles me a little bit because people can cope with voting for different political parties or supporting different football teams, but apparently religion is too delicate and too personal to criticise.

I was not going to write another line about the Church, but a few things started to bother me after I posted my blog. Someone I had known for years saw me in town, so naturally, I smiled and said hello, but they looked at me stone-faced and just turned away. Another friend I have and see around a lot does his best to steer clear. I wondered if this was all because of a single blog post. I do not ignore them because they still belong to the Church, so why disrespect me like that? Why should my lowly opinions about the Church affect their rock-solid testimonies, when they claim to 'know without a shadow of a doubt the Church is true'? Who cares what I think anymore, right? If it is all true, why does my little blog post matter? If they are free to worship how they want, am I not equally as free to have my say too?

It is perfectly okay in a Mormon mindset to critique my life, or the lives of all those who are less active, or non-members, perfectly fine to judge and label us as lost or unrighteous, but if I critique the religion, it is classed as mockery or apostatising.

Some members of the Church have approached me with words to this effect: 'I know you're still a good person, who lives a good life and will help people, and we still love you for that'. At first, I thought this was said with good intent, but now I realise it is just a backhanded compliment. What they really mean is, 'Even though you've taken a wrong path and lost the Spirit of God, I know you're still a good person.' What did they expect, me to get 666 tattooed on my forehead and start sacrificing goats to Satan while I wear a Slipknot mask? Did they expect to see videos of me doing lines of coke off of hookers' butt cheeks on social media? It is really patronising that they think I want to be told I am still a good person, by someone who has clearly put themselves above me on the morality chart. Would it be okay if I approached them with, 'Even though I think you're brainwashed and a tad delusional, I know you're still a good person'?

For decades, I walked around under a thick cloud of delusion, and it is only now that I can see things with any clarity. It is impossible for members to understand this because, and I do not mean this with any malice, they are still wandering around under that cloud.

I loved to believe that I could have a personal relationship with God and His son, that I could be guided by the Holy Ghost, protected and blessed by the priesthood, and hope for eternal life with all of my friends and family—what an amazing concept. Who would not want that to be true? The Church tells us where we come from, why we are here, and where we are going. All the great mysteries of life are solved. It has scriptures written by prophets that become heroes to the reader. I revered them all, especially Joseph Smith, and I will admit that even to this day, I miss believing they were legitimate. This is what I loved about the Church, but all the fear and guilt infected the good parts like a plague. I hoped for salvation, but fear always triumphed—fear that I am not going to make it, fear that I am not worthy enough, fear that I am not doing enough, fear that I am not forgiven for my sins, and fear that I cannot overcome my weakness. What a combination for control: fear and guilt to rule us while there is hope of heaven.

Some members have tried to re-awaken past experiences in me, trying to remind me of how I used to feel, so I want to lay down my thoughts on that too. I cannot deny that I used to refer to a warm, good, hopeful feeling as the Spirit, but the more I think about it, the more I realise that it does not confirm anything at all. Often leaders will say something along the lines of, 'Listen to this message, with a prayer in your heart'. Well, if the message is so true and insightful, why not just say, 'Listen to this message'? Of course, if you approach a message with a prayer in your heart, you have already conditioned your mind to receive it, so it will appear to have more of an impact. 'Dear Lord, please carry this message into my heart, help me feel the Spirit of it and understand it so that I can apply it to my life'; you have told your mind what do to with the message you are about to receive.

I mean, how can you not feel good about concepts you wish to be true? If you are reading scriptures about eternal life and you want it to be true, you will feel good. If you read about Christ healing the sick and raising the dead, you will feel inspired and uplifted. If you read about Christ's sacrifice for your sins, and you are feeling guilty about something you have done, you are going to feel humbled and repentant. If you combine that with the atmosphere of a quiet place of worship, with emotive hymns, you are going to be emotionally receptive to the environment.

I did feel that inner peace in situations like that, but I also felt that inner peace sitting quietly with my wife in a Buddhist temple in Japan. Also, testimony meetings at church always felt more spiritual than regular services because people were opening up to each other and sharing their thoughts and feelings, which created a bonding atmosphere. I used to think it was hyper-spiritual, but again, I have felt the same way when I have had heartfelt conversations with people I have just met over a beer.

People try to refer me back to how I used to feel, but I cannot rely on those feelings anymore. I labelled it as feeling the Spirit, but in reality, my own mind conjured up those emotions depending on the environment, or what I was bringing to the table. I wanted it to be true, so I felt it to be true. You cannot depend on that as solid testimony.

There were also times where I did pray for answers, insights, or comfort, and I got nothing. I will reiterate what I have said before: how can you trust prayer when it has a fifty-fifty chance of working? If I prayed to get a job, I am either going to get it or I am not. If I got it, I would attribute it to God for my prayer being answered; if not, I would file it away in the 'God knows best' folder.

I first started to realise that I was literally just speaking to myself in my head when I started to attend church less and less. I wanted God to come to me for a change, rather than me having to read my scriptures, sing hymns, pray, and live all the commandments. Again, doing all that makes your mind nice and ready for feeling connected to God because you have created the vibes.

When I wanted God to come to me, I was not reading the scriptures, or going to church, and guess what? I felt nothing. The Church will say that was because I removed myself from God, but there are countless examples in the scriptures where God has reached out to people when they have not earned it. Someone has told me that they received an angelic visitation while they were inactive and the angel told him to return to church. Did he tell me this to just win an argument or does he believe it? If he believes it then I respond with, 'Good for you, but where's my angel? Am I not as important to God? Why would he give you a taste of sure knowledge to nudge you back in the right direction and not to others?'

In the end, prayer became a torment for me. Straining all of my stressful thoughts and heart pangs out to the heavens only to be greeted with silence and an empty feeling can really give you a negative and combative attitude. Even the scriptures became a fair-weather friend. Of course, it is all well and good when you are cherry-picking all the lovely uplifting verses, but the racist, misogynistic, homophobic, and genocidal verses are a bit of a downer.

Maybe I am veering off course now, but maybe this will prevent people from just assuming that a failed mission or not having a baby were the reasons that I left the church.

The truth is I did feel brainwashed and conditioned to think the Mormon way for the best part of my life, and I have realised that it is not as easy as I thought to just move on and not feel angry. Although generally, I do just fine, until someone I know blanks me in the street because I have been outspoken, or until someone enforces their church opinions on me and then recoils when I shoot mine back. Maybe I am fine until I get patronised about still being a decent human being even though I am not a Mormon.

Members argue that the Church is perfect, but its people are not. Some people have said to me that it was imperfect people handling things badly throughout my church life that caused me more stress than I deserved. Yet even if that was the case, it is disturbing that people are allowed to be allocated influential positions that can cause an incredible amount of damage if abused. People are given advice regarding mental health, marriage, and general life problems by leaders that are not trained or qualified to do so. To be told not to question or criticise the brethren is the action of a dictatorship. This concept was so ingrained into me that I did not speak out against church leaders for over a decade after I came home from a mission.

The process of untangling the Church's sticky web was not easy. It took a lot of time to eradicate its guilt, which would creep up on me like a thief in the night as I began to change my thinking. It was also tough accepting that I no longer had the comfort of being one of God's elect children, chosen to hold the priesthood, and sealed to my family for time and all eternity. I do not rely on prayer or blessings when things go wrong anymore. I do not even have faith in an afterlife, which is perhaps the hardest pill to swallow; I hope there is, but I highly doubt it. I feel like I have been told that all my imaginary friends are not real and I am scared of being alone. I do not know anything for sure; perhaps I never will. I am sure that I will never be deceived by religion again. How can anyone trust that their religion is true when the chances are their faith is a result of geography and upbringing? Mormons born in Utah cannot really be objective. What if they had been born in Indonesia instead? Then, they would be saying that the Muslim faith is the only true faith in the world and *vice versa*. I just cannot allow myself to rely on people's feelings and testimonies as truth or fact. I could not even depend on my own. All I trust in now is what I actually know for sure. I am done relying on my gut to think for me; now, I use my brain and desire actual evidence lest I fall into deceit again. Losing my faith is not as bleak as I expected it to be either. Some people have expected me to be depressed and unhappy now that I have walked away from my faith, but there is a wonderful beauty in knowing that against all the odds, we are living on a sustainable planet in the vast expanse of space. Maybe we just have to find our own meanings and purposes in life; maybe that is enough.

Another question that has been put to me is, 'What if you are wrong?'

Even in the unlikely event that God does exist, would a supreme being really be so quick to anger, and be so easily offended by our trivial little earth activities? Do you really think a higher intelligence would care about me listening to Blink-182 or watching *Game of Thrones*? Would God frown at me for having a cup of tea? Does God really answer the prayers of privileged Mormon kids that have lost their BMW car keys, while ignoring starving children dying in the world? Why does God care what two people get up to in the bedroom? Why would the Holy Ghost be there like some disapproving voyeur anyway? If God is that pedantic, then I do not want to worship or serve Him anyway. If my family and friends are not going to make it either, then why would I want to spend eternity in a place with members that I did not even get along with on earth?

However, if there is a loving Father in Heaven, who is full of mercy and goodness, who loves His children beyond our comprehension, then will He not want to save us all in the end anyway? If He does not bring all of His children home, then is He not a failure as a father and a God? However, if God cannot save us all because He is bound by the laws of justice, then how supreme is He anyway? That means that eternal laws are more powerful, which just does not make any rational sense to me. If I am wrong, then can I really be held accountable when God hid behind the curtain the whole time? What if you are wrong, Mormons? You will have wasted your life on the word of a great con artist, or a deluded nut that you never even met. All I can do is accept life for what it is. No one knows anything for certain. Belief is not knowledge.

I just wish that people would stop being so easily offended and sensitive over insignificant standards and other people's life choices. If you want to be offended, be offended by world hunger or government corruption, be offended by global warming or illegal wars, be offended by unequal rights, animal cruelty, and domestic violence. Quit being so upset by people drinking beer or wearing bikinis. Morality is not exclusive to religion. I honestly believe that I am a better person today than I ever was as a Mormon. I am no longer judgemental and I am more accepting of alternative lifestyles and people who are different from me. I know Mormons will think that I have thrown away my salvation and rebelled against God. I know they think that I will not make it to their celestial kingdom, but that reality only exists in their minds—just because they think it does not make it true.

A recent talk by a Latter-day Saint apostle asked the following questions to the Church: 'If you choose to become inactive or to leave the restored Church of Jesus Christ of Latter-day Saints, where will you go? What will you do?' I have chosen to leave the Church and I will go wherever my free-thinking mind wants to go, and do whatever my free-thinking mind wants to do.

Do not live out your one life for anyone else. This is not a video game; you are not going to get a second chance. Stop wasting time beating yourselves up and instead do what makes you happy. Just do not be a dick.

Epilogue

When I completed the manuscript for this book, I announced it on social media. Many people were excited and offered me their support and good wishes, but some members of the Church contacted me, telling me to be careful and to be mindful that because I still have Mormon friends, I ought to be respectful of their beliefs.

The very day I announced the book title, someone tried hacking into my Facebook account. It may well be a coincidence, but I have never had this happen to my account since I first made it. If I had to hazard a guess, I think someone either wanted to see if they could find any samples in my private inbox because the book title itself hints at temple exposure, or they just wanted to mess with me. Either way, it made me paranoid, but I used to believe the closest star to heaven was called Kolob, so forgive the ridiculous notions I have from time to time.

I had not even found a publisher yet, but the rumblings had already begun. Someone I have known for over twenty years, who my family has given time, money, and support to, decided to unfriend us all on social media without even a word, all because we have left the Church and promoted this book. One guy contacted my dad and asked what our agenda was. He went so ridiculously over the top he asked if we would end up wanting to round Mormons up at gun point to put them in some kind of concentration camp. I have seen so many patronising and ignorant comments from people about this book despite the fact that they have not read it because it was not even out. Several people I have known for years also unfriended me because they see this book as apostasy and anti-Mormon literature. I do not believe this book fits into either of those categories, so, in closing, I wanted to reiterate the purpose of this book because people have asked me why I have written it. It is my personal story with Mormonism, the views and opinions expressed within are mine and mine alone. My humour can be crass and irreverent, but no one needs to take that personally.

Members still send my family Church talks and scripture passages to read even though it is unwelcome. If I sent them Richard Dawkins books in return, they would be outraged and say it was disrespectful. This is clearly a double standard. If you are free to write testimony to me, then I should be equally free to write this book. I have not written it for the purpose of persuading people to leave the Church, or not to join it, but because there was interest in my story and I hoped that it could help someone else who feels that it relates to them.

If anyone recognises themselves in this book and I have put your nose out of joint, please know that I am not holding onto grudges or ill feelings, but like it or not, you are part of my story with Mormonism.

You can choose not to be offended if you want. Mormon apostle Elder Bednar, said so: 'You and I cannot control the intentions or behavior of other people. However, we do determine how we will act. Please remember that you and I are agents endowed with moral agency, and we can choose not to be offended'. (*And Nothing Shall Offend Them*, October 2006)

People have asked me if writing this book has been a therapeutic experience for me. It has not been. I spent a few weeks really depressed by it. It opened up old wounds and my journal entries really shocked me. I do not even know that person anymore. I forgot that the writer of those books used to be me. I am still thinking about burning my journals because I do not think I can ever face looking at them again. I may well regret publishing extracts from them too because it is humiliating, but if I can just convince one or two people reading this book not to torture themselves over religious guilt, then perhaps the embarrassment I feel will be worth it. I am sorry if this book was a heavy read. If you stuck with it, then thank you for your patience.

In closing, I need my Mormon friends to know that there is no void in my life now I have rejected the Church. I have not rejected you as people, but the organisation itself is not for me. Do not worry about my soul or my salvation either. I am happy to eventually just die and see what is on the other side. If there is a loving God that wants to talk to me, I will take my chances with Her/Him/It/Them directly. If there is not, then I won't know any different and I will finally be free of all the bullshit in the world. An eternal sleep is not such a bad concept for me; sure, I would love to be in paradise with my loved ones forever, but I would also like to be smashing in match winners for Liverpool. We cannot have it all. For now, I am just happy to be enjoying my life as a free-thinker, unburdened by the restrictions of organised religion.

Should new evidence be found, which unlocks the great mysteries of the universe, then I am open-minded enough to change my position. I wish people of faith would also be that versatile. When you think about it, The Church of Jesus Christ of Latter-day Saints claims to be the one true church. That means that they think that every other religion in the world is wrong. All I have done is add one more religion to that pile. Other Christians have tried to convert me to their theologies now that I have stepped away from Mormonism, but why would I jump out of the frying pan and into the fire? If other people find legitimate happiness in their faith, then that is brilliant, but as for me, I am done with it all.

Sixteen years have passed since I was in Roseville, California. I am thirty-five years old now, and I still have nightmares that I am back on a mission trying to be obedient and trying desperately to get home.